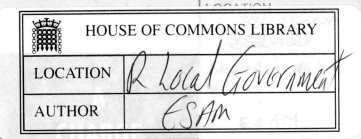
A CHARGE ON THE COMMUNITY

THE POLL TAX BENEFITS AND THE POOR

Peter

Esam

and

Carey

Oppenheim

CHILD
POVERTY
ACTION
GROUP

LGIU

The views expressed in this book do not necessarily represent the official policy of the Child Poverty Action Group, or of all local authorities and trade unions who sponsor the Local Government Information Unit.

British Library Cataloguing in Publication Data

Esam, Peter
   A charge on the community: the poll tax,
   benefits and the poor
   1. England. Rates. Replacement by poll tax,
      1660-1664. Taxpayers. Lists
   I. Title II. Oppenheim, Carey,
   III. Child Poverty Action Group/Local Government Information Unit
   336.22′0942

   ISBN 0-946744-16-5

Cover design and artwork by Clifford Harper
Typeset by Nancy White
Artwork by Boldface Typesetters
Printed by Calvert's Press

Contents

Acknowledgements

We would like to thank our readers for their helpful comments: Fran Bennett, Archie Fairley, Peter Golding, John Hills, Judy Mallaber, David Piachaud, Albert Tait, Tony Travers and Holly Sutherland. We owe a particular debt of gratitude to Holly Sutherland, who not only offered advice about our use of 'Taxmod', but also adapted the model to make our analysis possible. We are also grateful to John Hills, who gave us access to the data he used for modelling tax and benefit changes since 1978/79 in his book, *Changing Tax* (CPAG Ltd, 1989). Thanks to Judith Arnit, Lynda Bransbury, David Lancefield and Geoff Fimister for guidance on drafting the questionnaire to local authorities. Many thanks to the local authorities who filled in the questionnaires and to the people who administered them on our behalf. Nicki Simpson at the National Association of Citizens' Advice Bureaux (NACAB) provided access to NACAB's very useful case studies. Ian Douglas helped us with advice and material. Our thanks to Richard Kennedy who indexed the book, and especially to Nancy White for her ingenious and accurate typesetting of the manuscript. Finally, many thanks to Julia Lewis for all her work on preparing the manuscript for publication.

The time devoted to researching and writing this book stretched the patience of our work colleagues, and we are grateful to them for all their support.

Foreword

After months of controversy, poll tax (community charge) payments have started in Scotland and the first bills go out in early 1990 in England and Wales. The poll tax has arrived — yet the debate about it continues.

For the government, it is a fair tax because everyone pays the same. The government also claims that it provides a flat-rate 'price' for local government services, ostensibly enabling local voters to see easily what value they get from their local councils.

Opponents of the poll tax argue that it is unfair, redistributing the tax burden further from rich to poor; and that the poll tax — with the accompanying changes to the grant system and business rates — is designed to make local authorities cut their spending on local services.

It has become increasingly clear to CPAG and LGIU, from their distinct and different perspectives, that an accurate analysis of the impact of the poll tax also has to include an examination of the changes in the social security system fully implemented in 1988 under the 1986 Social Security Act.

First, it was through this Act that the government started to introduce the idea that local authorities would be more 'accountable' if everyone — no matter how poor — paid something towards local taxation. Since April 1988, those on subsistence level benefits have had to pay 20% of their rates bill — and this has been carried through to the poll tax. Analysis of whether income support levels provide adequate compensation for this payment must be part of looking at how poorer families fare under the poll tax. It is also one area where we can already start to see the serious impact of recent changes in practice.

Second, the government argues that the cost of local services should not be hidden by allowing those on lower incomes to pay a lower poll tax. Instead, it says, help for the poorest to pay the poll tax should be provided explicitly through the social security system via poll tax rebates. The government argues that rebates ensure that the poll tax is a fair tax. But poll tax rebates are only one part of the changes in the social security system, which are meant to be part of a package to simplify benefits and target resources on those most in need. Analysis of the distributional impact of the 1986 Social Security

Act must go hand in hand with examining subsequent changes through poll tax rebates and the poll tax itself.

Third, the government argues that the 1988 social security changes were geared to help those most in need (a claim which has been challenged by a wide range of organisations). Yet the government never subjected subsequent changes to benefits and taxes (including the poll tax) to this test; indeed, in many cases they have had the opposite effect. It is inconsistent of the government to use such a test for one set of policies, yet fail to follow this through to related policies of equal importance to those on lower incomes.

Fourth, local authorities have been given increasing responsibility for administering benefits on behalf of the government — notably with the transfer of housing benefit. Councils now make many welfare payments, set and collect the poll tax and provide welfare services — all with a major impact on the distribution of income in their communities. The combined impact will inevitably affect the way in which local people view their relationship with their local authority. The social security and poll tax legislation present local authorities with a real dilemma. In order to provide welfare benefits and services to those most in need, they have to impose a flat-rate tax on those least able to afford it. Councils need to know the precise impact of their actual or potential actions in these areas.

The sweeping changes to social security and local government finance have thus brought together the interests of CPAG and LGIU. For CPAG, its traditional concern with the position of low-income families has led it to look beyond an emphasis on benefits and to focus in recent publications on the interaction between benefits and taxation, including the poll tax. From a local government perspective, LGIU has looked at recent legislation to see how effective local services and welfare provision can be maintained and improved, particularly to assist the disadvantaged — an aim put in jeopardy by the changes examined in this publication.

We therefore decided to undertake a systematic statistical analysis, bringing together the effects of the 1986 Social Security Act, the poll tax (including the rebates system) and changes to direct taxation. This publication analyses the distributional impact on various income bands, by region, by sex and by race. Even on the most cautious assumptions about the likely levels of poll tax, the computer analysis shows that recent changes have benefited the rich and left the poor relatively worse off.

The publication also unravels the government's arguments on accountability and dependency, and shows how similar themes underlie all these 'reforms'. As far as people on low incomes are concerned, it shows how the changes in general mean less power and more bureaucracy. The authors look at the room for manoeuvre left to local authorities seeking to serve the needs of their communities, and make proposals for the policies which are needed to strengthen the local provision of welfare in the 1990s.

As this new legislation is implemented, many people will be interested in investigations of its impact. We believe that *A Charge on the Community* provides the first comprehensive analysis and discussion of the combined impact on lower income groups of two of the most substantial legislative initiatives in social policy of the late 1980s. Both organisations believe that the very disturbing findings in this publication show the urgent need for progressive and well-founded alternative policies to ensure genuine local democracy and fairness.

Fran Bennett, Director, Child Poverty Action Group
Judy Mallaber, Director, Local Government Information Unit

Introduction

A massive upheaval took place in the social security system in 1988 —
particularly affecting people on the lowest incomes. Heralded as the
most important reform since Beveridge, the Social Security Act 1986
has tilted the social security system firmly in the direction of means
testing. 1988 also marked the beginning of a radical restructuring of
local authority finance: registration for the poll tax began in Scotland
and the Local Government Finance Act 1988 for England and Wales
was passed.[1] The poll tax is now a reality.

When the government evaluates the effects of major changes such
as these, it tends to look at them in isolation — and not very compre-
hensively at that. Thus the government's defence of the April 1988
social security changes has relied heavily on one statistic, as the Rt
Hon John Moore MP, Secretary of State for Social Security, made
clear in a speech to the Commons:

> The overwhelming majority of recipients — 88 per cent of them, and that
> is the true figure — will receive at least as much as they did before.[2]

This figure was based on a comparison of cash incomes before and
after April 1988 — so it counted any increase in benefit as a 'gain'
even if the increase was less than the rate of inflation and involved a
cut in the *real* income of the claimant. The figure included 'transitional
protection' (a temporary supplement to ordinary benefit, which is
already being phased out) but ignored the loss of single payments
(lump-sum grants for special needs).[3] So, even though the figure used
by ministers is literally true, the reliance upon it indicates a reluctance
to present an overall analysis of the consequences of the social security
changes and to defend government policy on that basis.

A more comprehensive evaluation is therefore desirable. Moreover,
it is also useful to put the two sets of government measures — the
poll tax and the recent social security changes — together, and to
attempt to describe their *cumulative* effect. For those on low incomes
the cumulative impact may be greater or less than the effects in
isolation: a cut in benefit of £1 a week may become a loss of £2 when
the poll tax is due — or in some cases it may be cancelled out by a
gain. We need to evaluate these effects. For local authorities there is

the concern that an accumulation of poverty may place additional pressure on social services; and that, having been given the job of administering the recent cuts in housing benefit, they must now also collect the poll tax.

Nor is the full impact on individuals confined to cash gains or losses, vitally important though these are. The poll tax is intended by the government to reduce the level of services — encouraging voters to look less favourably on local authority expenditure. Yet those on low incomes rely on the welfare state for services they cannot afford to purchase, as well as for cash benefits. So it is important to analyse the cumulative impact of a series of reforms which affect both the distribution of incomes and the provision of services. Moreover, the radical restructuring of social security and local government taxation involves new administrative arrangements, and new forms of relationship between the individual and officialdom.

So in this book one of our main objectives is to assess the overall impact on low-income groups of recent legislative changes in the fields of social security and local government finance. We also want to look at these changes from the perspective of local authorities — to assess the impact on local authorities' role in social security provision, their capacity to fund services (particularly in areas of high deprivation), and their relationship with deprived and vulnerable sections of their communities. A third objective is to suggest what policy changes are necessary both at central and local level. How should local authorities respond to central government policies, bearing in mind the need to protect vulnerable groups? What alternatives are there to the poll tax?

Of course, recent changes in central government taxation are also relevant to a cumulative analysis, because they have directly altered the overall distribution of incomes. Moreover, an analysis which ignored cuts in direct taxation would be open to criticism for failing to take account of gains which may have accrued to those who are worst off. To guard against this kind of partiality, we take account of changes to direct taxation when we assess the effects of government policies on living standards. But we do not enter into any analysis of taxation policy — to do so would take us beyond the scope of this book.[4]

How do we judge the impact of the poll tax and social security changes? Some of the key objectives which should underpin reform are relatively uncontroversial, especially in relation to those on the lowest incomes. For example, it seems obvious that policies should aim to protect the living standards of the worst off — and wherever possible to improve them. Similarly, these policies should aim to give the poor more control over their own lives and more power in relation to the state — whether that means Department of Social Security officials or local authorities.

Interestingly enough, the themes which government ministers have relied upon in defending the impact on low-income groups of both the social security changes and the poll tax have much in common. Firstly, they have argued that means-tested benefits are an effective way of providing for the needs of low-income groups. In relation to the social security changes, ministers have argued that means-tested benefits are a more effective way of targeting scarce resources than universal flat-rate benefits, and that they will provide adequate protection for the poor when the value of universal benefits is cut. The poll tax is, of course, a universal flat-rate tax: here the government argues that means-tested rebates can protect the poor by relating the actual poll tax due to ability to pay. In both fields it is argued that means-tested benefits can protect the poorest from extra costs: for example, the costs of increased rents, higher prices for school meals or poll tax payments.

Secondly, the government has argued that in different ways its policies have given more power and control to individuals. The Rt Hon John Moore MP, Secretary of State for Social Security, has argued that the government's social security reforms are bringing about greater independence for the poor by reducing 'welfare dependency'. In large part this argument rests on the idea that if the scope of state activity can be curtailed, then individual initiative will be freed. On the poll tax the argument is more complex. One of the central objectives of the new tax is to promote 'accountability', an objective which implies greater control over the activities of local authorities being exercised by individual voters. But there is also a subsidiary theme: ministers have suggested that voters do not really want the level of services currently provided, and that improved accountability will entail a shrinking of local government. As with social security, this retrenchment of state welfare is seen as enhancing the power of individuals to pursue their own independent objectives.

The success of these policies depends crucially on the adequacy of means-tested benefits to fulfil the tasks assigned to them by the government. Firstly, the question of living standards: are these benefits capable in practice of protecting the poor from cuts in living standards due to the restructuring of social security and local government taxation? Secondly, the question of administrative adequacy: can they be claimed without losing the dignity and independence which it is the government's declared aim to promote?

No better method could have been devised than the poll tax to test the belief that means-tested benefits can compensate for the effects of social policies which would otherwise bear down unreasonably on poor people. Being flat-rate, the tax is unrelated to ability to pay over ranges of income where rebates are not payable. Moreover, the tax entangles anyone unable to pay in a maze of bureaucratic checks,

court orders and enforcement remedies. Finally, there is the threat to
services: how will the needs of people on low incomes be met if, as
ministers anticipate, local services do indeed shrink?

In this book we put these concerns about the likely impact of the
poll tax alongside the actual experience of the social security changes
introduced in April 1988. We ask whether the new social security
system provides a secure base from which people on low incomes can
face the prospect of the poll tax with equanimity, or whether they
must fear that one cut in their standard of living is to be swiftly
followed by another. We also locate these concerns in the context of
the local authority role in welfare. Despite the general hostility of
central government to the direct provision of services by local authorities, local government continues to play a major (and in some
instances a growing) role in the provision both of social security
benefits and of welfare services such as education and support for the
elderly. One of the purposes of this book is to assess the implications
of the major changes which are taking place in the fields of social
security and local government finance for this local provision of
welfare. Are local authorities still able to find a space in which to
promote welfare locally, or is their room for manoeuvre becoming
impossibly constrained?

In Chapter 1 we examine the changing role of local authorities in
welfare provision and the importance of locally provided services and
benefits to low-income households. In Chapter 2 we describe the
recent social security changes and the poll tax. This is a purely
descriptive chapter. Those already familiar with the legislative
changes described may wish to move straight on to Chapter 3.

In Chapter 3 we lay out the government's objectives in the reform
of social security and local government finance, which it argues
promote independence and accountability. In Chapter 4 we examine
the impact of the introduction in April 1988 of a minimum contribution to the rates (of 20 per cent) payable by income support
claimants. We draw on examples from the National Association of
Citizens' Advice Bureaux records, and on the results of our own small
survey of local authorities.

In Chapter 5 we assess the strengths and weaknesses of the government's case for targeting benefits on low-income families through
means-tested benefits and evaluate the impact of the social security
and tax changes on living standards. To do this we use a computer
model ('Taxmod') developed at the London School of Economics.

In Chapter 6 we examine the impact of the poll tax on living
standards in two stages. We also look at the impact of the poll tax on
women and on black and other ethnic minorities. In Chapter 7 we
look at the cumulative effect of the April 1988 social security changes,
the April 1988 Budget, and the introduction of the poll tax. We build

up a picture of the way the changes interact — and, to complete the picture, we include a comparison with the tax and benefit system of 1978/79.

Chapter 8 focuses on the changes to local government finance in more detail and the impact of these on the more deprived regions and nations in Great Britain. Chapter 9 concentrates on the poll tax and deprivation in individual local authorities in England and Scotland. We look at how the poll tax can be expected to affect the capacity of local authorities in deprived areas to fund services.

In Chapter 10 we ask whether the combined effect of the recent social security changes and the poll tax is indeed to give more power to individuals in their dealings with the state.

In Chapter 11 we look at the policy conclusions which can be drawn from our analysis. We suggest ways in which local authorities should respond to central government policies, and argue for a set of principles which could underpin an alternative to the poll tax. Chapter 12 sums up our arguments and conclusions.

Notes
1 The poll tax is not being introduced in Northern Ireland.
2 Speech by the Rt Hon John Moore MP, 23 April 1988.
3 See Chapter 2 for a full explanation of the social security changes.
4 For a thorough analysis of taxation policy since 1979 and its effects, see John Hills, *Changing Tax: How the tax system works and how to change it*, CPAG Ltd, 1989.

1 Local welfare in the 1980s

The Social Security Act 1986 and the poll tax strike at the heart of local authorities' power to fund and deliver benefits and services. This chapter analyses why locally provided welfare is crucial to low-income groups and how it has changed over the last ten years.

The role of local authorities in welfare

The government is widely perceived as wishing to restrict the role of local authorities in service provision. The model local authority is seen by Conservative ministers as 'enabling not providing'.[1] Yet, taking a broad view of welfare — to include education, personal social services, health and social security — local authorities are responsible for over a quarter of welfare state expenditure. Moreover, the share of welfare spending for which local authorities are responsible has not diminished in recent years: indeed, largely due to the transfer of housing benefit to local authorities in 1982/83, there has been a slight increase.[2] In 1979/80 local authority current expenditure on welfare services was 23.9 per cent of central government current expenditure on welfare services; it is predicted that by 1990/91 it will be 25.3 per cent. Local authorities themselves are devoting more of their own current expenditure to welfare — in 1979/80, 64.8 per cent of current local authority expenditure went on welfare; the figure is projected to rise to 70.2 per cent in 1990/91.[3]

The distribution of welfare services

Although services are not as redistributive as cash benefits, they are of great importance to the living standards of low-income households. The Central Statistical Office (CSO) makes annual assessments of the relative importance of welfare services and cash benefits to different income groups[4] (see table 1.1). The 'benefits in kind' that it examines are: education, health services, subsidies for housing and transport, and free school meals and milk. The calculations include both national and local services, but do not cover personal social services, because of the difficulty of estimating their usage. Local authorities are primarily responsible for spending in three of the services considered — education, housing and free school meals/milk — and are also responsible for a substantial proportion of spending in a fourth (transport).

Expenditure on services for non-retired households is distributed roughly equally between income groups. Housing subsidies are weighted towards the worst-off (mortgage interest tax relief is accounted for separately), but this effect is cancelled out by the greater benefit which affluent households derive from travel subsidies. Spending on school meals and milk is of greatest benefit to the poorest households, but the biggest items — education and health — are roughly evenly spread.

However, an even spread of expenditure between the income groups in fact means that these services are of disproportionate benefit to low-income households, as table 1.1 shows. Households are ranked according to income and divided into five approximately equal groups ('quintiles'). The bottom quintile includes the 20 per cent of households with the lowest incomes, and the top quintile the 20 per cent of households with the highest incomes.

Table 1.1   Average value of benefits in kind for each quintile group (non-retired households ranked by original income) 1986

	Quintile group					
	Bottom	2nd	3rd	4th	Top	Total
£ per household per annum						
Education	930	710	840	850	870	840
National health service	680	680	730	680	730	700
Housing subsidy	140	60	40	30	10	60
Travel subsidies	30	50	40	60	110	60
School meals and milk	110	30	30	20	20	40
Total	1900	1540	1680	1640	1730	1700
Benefits in kind as a percentage of post-tax[1] income	60	32	24	17	10	20

1   Income after cash benefits and all taxes

Source: *Economic Trends,* Central Statistical Office, December 1988

NB: No account of cuts to the school meals service in April 1988 is included in the above table, and so the importance of that component will have declined since the period covered by the study. The education figure is also distorted by the fact that the bottom income group contains the largest number of students — for whom the costs of education are greatest.

The less well-off households rely far more heavily on services as a component of their living standards: the relevant 'benefits in kind' add 60 per cent to the post-tax income (income after cash benefits and all taxes) of the bottom quintile, and 32 per cent to that of the second quintile. This compares with a mere 10 per cent added to the post-tax income of households in the top quintile by these services. The position is similar for retired households: 'benefits in kind' add 68 per cent to the post-tax income of the bottom quintile, whereas for the top quintile the figure is only 17 per cent.[5]

A recent study by Glen Bramley, Julian Le Grand and William Low[6] casts a different light on the problem. They studied some 70 per cent of the expenditure incurred by one county council, Cheshire, and found that most services were either distributed in equal measure to the top and bottom income groups (quintiles) or benefited the poorest group.[7] However, the heavy bias of expenditure on a few items (post-16 and adult education, roads, parks, libraries and waste tips) meant that in absolute terms the top income group gained more from council services than the bottom group. The top quintile received 25.6 per cent of services by value, whereas the bottom quintile received only 16.1 per cent.

However, this study does not invalidate the conclusions drawn from the CSO analysis. It is not possible to generalise over the whole spectrum of local authorities from one example; in particular, as its authors note, metropolitan areas may well have a different distribution of services. The study takes no account of spending at district level, including spending on housing and housing benefit. Nonetheless, the study does raise important questions about who benefits from local authority services, which we return to in the penultimate chapter.

The CSO's assumption that the benefits of welfare services are evenly spread between income groups stands up sufficiently well for our purposes. Even if an adjustment to the absolute value of service received by each income group were justified, the main finding of the CSO analysis — that services make up a far greater proportion of final income for lower-income groups — would still be accurate. Thus services, and in particular local authority services, are vital to the living standards of the poor. Education, housing, transport and school meals are all areas in which local authorities have major spending responsibilities. The capacity of local authorities to fund service provision is therefore of central importance to the role of the welfare state in providing services to those who cannot afford to purchase them on the open market.

New initiatives

Local authorities have been responsible for many initiatives in the

1980s aimed at meeting the particular needs of deprived and vulnerable sections of the community. Some local authorities have taken heed of criticisms of inflexibility and have made many productive efforts to provide services which are more responsive to local need. Increased effort and resources have been directed at areas such as equal opportunities, economic development and decentralisation of services.

The developing partnership between local authorities and the voluntary sector is a good example. Voluntary organisations often provide a range of vital services, particularly in areas of deprivation — from information and advice centres to transport for people with disabilities. In the 1980s local authorities have increasingly recognised the value of services provided by voluntary organisations, and by 1986/87 local authority funding was running at a level of £402 million — well over three times as much in cash terms as in 1982/83.[8]

Local authorities have also devoted increased resources to welfare rights work, with the specific intention of improving living standards for low-income residents. The success of some local authority welfare rights work was in part responsible for the greatly increased take-up of single payments during the 1980s.[9] These were lump-sum grants for special needs payable under the old supplementary benefit scheme but abolished under the 1986 Social Security Act. The number of payments increased from 830,000 in 1981 to 2.65 million in 1987.

The government response

Bearing in mind the importance of their services to those most in need, local authorities have struggled to maintain levels of provision during the 1980s. However, the government's policy has been to bring about a reduction in local authority expenditure. Since 1978/79, central government has cut £916 million in real terms from the total amount of its grant paid to local authorities in England.[10] Rate-capping was introduced, giving central government new powers which have been used to limit expenditure in some of the most deprived areas. In addition, authorities which spend above levels considered reasonable by central government have suffered punitive losses of grant, through a rigorous system of grant penalties. These policies have made it very difficult for authorities to fund improvements in the quality or quantity of services — and in many cases cuts in provision have occured.

At times the government's policies have also directly curtailed the capacity of local authorities to implement new approaches to service provision. For example, the Greater London Council and the Metropolitan Counties were at the forefront of policy innovation. They were also extremely active in funding voluntary organisations. Local authority funding of the voluntary sector has fallen slightly since

1985/86, a fact which the Charities Aid Foundation partly attributes to the abolition of these authorities.[11]

There is now concern over whether the poll tax can provide adequate revenue for services (see Chapters 8 and 9). Firstly, because it is a flat-rate tax which falls proportionately more heavily on the poor than on the rich, local authorities are faced with a dilemma: funding services — which are vitally important to people on low incomes — involves a *disproportionate* burden of taxation on those very same groups.[12] Secondly, the entire burden of increasing expenditure (or sustaining it in the face of cuts in revenue from other sources) will fall on poll tax payers, because local authorities will no longer control the level of income they receive from business rate-payers (see Chapter 2 for a full explanation). This means that the poll tax will have to increase disproportionately to fund extra services, or to cover shortfalls in income from government grants or the business rate: this is known as the problem of 'gearing'.

Local authorities and social security

Local authorities' principal social security responsibility is housing benefit. Housing benefit's recent history is of particular interest both as an illustration of local authorities' changing role in social security and also because poll tax rebates are modelled closely on the housing benefit scheme. Thus the changes to housing benefit provide a fore-taste of how poll tax rebates may operate in practice.

The transfer of housing benefit has meant that the proportion of spending on social security administered by local authorities has increased in the 1980s (for an explanation of the transfer, see note 2). Table 1.2 shows how housing benefit expenditure has more than tripled since it was phased in, and increased more than sevenfold in real terms over the whole period since 1979.

This increasing proportion of spending administered by local authorities is not an indication of increased generosity in the rules of entitlement. Far from it. Ever since housing benefit was introduced, with the associated increase in the role of local authorities, it has borne the brunt of central government social security cuts (see table 1.3). Moreover, where local authorities have had discretion to pay addi-tional benefit or to apply the statutory rules generously, central government has tended to intervene to curtail discretionary powers, or to penalise the beneficial use of such powers through restrictions in the subsidies it pays to local authorities.[13]

The right of local authorities to run their own local housing benefit 'top-up' schemes was abolished in April 1988, with the exception of extra help to people with war disabilities and war widows.[14] This step

Table 1.2   Social security expenditure at the local level in Great Britain
1978/79 to 1990/91

	Amount of local authority expenditure (£ million at 1987-88 prices)	Proportion of total social security expenditure (%)
1978-79	540	1.6
1979-80	530	1.6
1980-81	580	1.7
1981-82	790	2.1
1982-83[1]	1,300	3.2
1983-84[1]	3,060	7.3
1984-85	3,320	7.6
1985-86	3,460	7.7
1986-87	3,620	7.8
1987-88[2]	3,760	8.1
1988-89[2]	3,830	8.3
1989-90[2]	3,920	8.3
1990-91[2]	4,020	8.4

Source: *House of Commons Hansard*, 14 November 1988, col 459.

1   These increases reflect the introduction of the housing benefit scheme, which transferred responsibility for the housing costs of supplementary benefit claimants from central government to local authorities.
2   Figures for 1987-88 to 1990-91 are based on those published in January 1988 in the public expenditure White Paper, Cmnd 288.

was taken despite the fact that the costs of the schemes fell on local ratepayers, not central government. At the same time a restrictive limit was placed on expenditure on discretionary housing benefit payments made to individuals in exceptional circumstances[15] (the power to make such payments is being removed for poll tax rebates). Subsidy rules were also changed to penalise authorities which backdate benefit or pay housing benefit for properties with high rents or accommodation 'larger than is reasonably required' by the claimant. More recently, government measures have forced local authorities to apply their limited discretion even more stringently. For example, in 1989 the government issued guidelines to define the concept of unreasonably large accommodation more precisely — an authority would lose subsidy for paying a rent rebate to a family which has a room each for a boy and a girl under 10 years old.[16]

Given this history of cuts and restrictions, how is it that local

Table 1.3   Housing benefit savings 1983-1988

Date of change	Amount saved (£ million)[1]
April 1983	(approx) 50
April and November 1984	171[2]
April 1985	6
November 1985	57[3]
July 1986	26
April 1987	68
April 1988	620[4]

Source: *House of Commons Hansard*, 25 November 1987, col 247; *House of Commons Hansard*, 25 February 1988, col 301.

1   All savings are shown in terms of the full-year effects and include savings in rate rebate expenditure, which is not formally classified as public expenditure. The savings for different years cannot be aggregated over a period because the effects of the changes overlap and are partly offset by other factors.
2   This figure is the estimated full-year cost in November 1984 of restoring the November 1983 tapers, minima, and equivalent levels for non-dependant deductions and the dependent child's needs allowance.
3   This figure was offset by extra expenditure of £12 million resulting from the real increase in the child's needs allowance (net saving £45 million).
4   The £650 million saving was reduced very slightly by the government's concession to increase the capital limit for housing benefit from £6,000 to £8,000.

authority spending on social security has grown since 1978/79? Part of the growth is due to the same factors which underlie the increase in social security spending generally: increased unemployment, larger numbers of elderly people, one-parent families and disabled people, and the growth of poverty. However, in addition, the housing benefit scheme has been used to mop up the effects of cuts in direct housing investment and support (see table 1.4).

Central government investment in local authority housing has declined substantially: subsidies to local authorities were cut by 77 per cent over the nine-year period from 1978/79. Public subsidies to other sectors have not been increased in compensation: those to new towns have been heavily cut, while housing association subsidies have remained roughly constant. In response, local authorities have been compelled to raise their rents, which in turn has been partly responsible for forcing up spending on housing benefit: by 145 per cent between 1978/79 and 1987/88. Thus there has been a shift in the role of local government in housing, away from being a provider of homes and towards being the administrator of benefits. At the same time the cuts in housing investment have also led to increased homelessness and a consequent growth of expensive emergency provision in the form of board and lodging and temporary accommodation, much of it funded by local authorities without the assistance of central government subsidy.

Table 1.4 Public expenditure on housing subsidies and housing benefit and average local authority rents

| | General subsidies to: (£ million, 1987-88 prices[1]) | | | Housing benefit[5] expenditure 1987-88 prices £ million | Average local authority rents (England) 1987-88 prices £ per annum |
	Local authorities[2]	New towns[3]	Housing associations[4]		
1978-79	2,060	179	39	1,480	612
1979-80	2,237	177	42	1,390	581
1980-81	2,106	169	40	1,540	630
1981-82	1,224	158	49	2,110	796
1982-83	674	147	57	2,690	875
1983-84	336	143	30	3,020	864
1984-85	394	137	23	3,260	867
1985-86	444	98	27	3,400	865
1986-87	561	89	30	3,540	884
1987-88	473	83	36	3,620	895
% rise/fall between 1978/79 & 1987/88	−77%	−54%	−8%	+145%	+46%

Sources: *House of Commons Hansard*, 31 October 1988, cols 541-2 and cols 493-4; 27 June 1988, col 160; 3 November 1988, col 735; 15 February 1989, col 236.

1 Using GDP deflator.
2 Primarily Main Housing subsidy, which is paid to local authorities in support of provision, repair and maintenance of their rented stock, does not include rate fund contributions.
3 Similar to 2, but paid in support of New Town housing.
4 Revenue grants and subsidies to housing associations: revenue deficit grant; hostel deficit grant; and grant affording relief from income tax, profits tax and corporation tax. Does not include capital grants to housing associations (HAG).
5 Housing benefit refers to housing costs for SB claimants and rent rebates and allowances prior to the introduction of the new HB scheme in 1982/83. It excludes rate rebates.

Figure 1.1 illustrates the dramatic change over the last ten years in the way housing expenditure funded by central government is allocated. At the beginning of the decade the majority of such funding came in the form of subsidies to assist in the provision of housing by local authorities, housing associations and New Towns. By the end of the decade the position is completely reversed: the vast majority of such spending is now devoted to housing benefit, and less than 15 per cent now goes to fund the direct provision of homes.

Figure 1.1   Shares of central government housing expenditure devoted to subsidies and to benefits 1978/79-1987/88

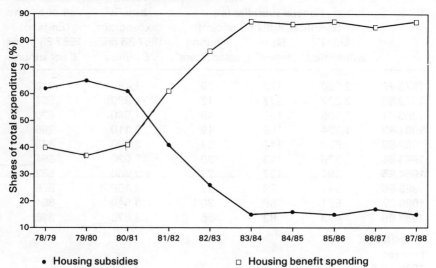

- Housing subsidies   □ Housing benefit spending

Sources: As in table 1.4
Notes: Housing subsidies are the total of columns 1 to 3 in table 1.4. Housing
         benefit expenditure is column 5 in table 1.4. Total 'housing' expenditure is
         the total of expenditure on subsidies and housing benefits (excluding rate
         rebates and allowances).

The growth in housing benefit expenditure has occurred despite the very large cuts in entitlement over the same period (see table 1.3): plainly, without these cuts, spending would have had to rise considerably higher. Yet with unfortunate irony this increase in expenditure — in large part a consequence of government policies — has itself been cited as a reason for cutting entitlement. Shortly after the full introduction of housing benefit in April 1983, the government announced cuts of £230 million. Following a public outcry these cuts were reduced to £185 million. This is how the DSS justified the cuts:

> Expenditure on rent and rate rebates has more than doubled in real terms since 1972... Nearly 40 per cent of the population now gets the benefit. Against this background, we believe it is perfectly reasonable to seek a modest reduction of less than 5 per cent in assistance with housing costs.[17]

Similar arguments were used in the 1985 Green Paper on the Reform of Social Security:

> We must avoid constructing systems, such as we now have in housing benefit, which grow from schemes designed to give help to those most in need until they cover much wider areas of the population. We must target the resources we have more effectively.[18]

The logic seems to be that if policies cause an increase in the level of need then the definition of need should be changed — not the policies.

The process seems set to continue with the implementation of the Housing Act 1988 which imposes market rents on new private and housing association tenants, to be followed by the Local Government and Housing Finance Bill (1989) which aims to do the same for local authority housing. Moreover, under the latter Bill housing benefit costs are to fall on local authority housing revenue accounts: this means that local authorities will be compelled to increase rents in in order to fund benefit payments. Those who lose will be the council tenants who are not eligible for rebates — a system which seems likely to create divisions between council tenants.

It would appear that central government has been happy to leave local authorities with responsibilities in the social security field — and in some cases to increase those responsibilities — because local authorities then attract much of the blame for inadequacies of provision, especially when that provision is cut. This view is consistent with the way that housing benefit and the free school meals service run by local authorities were severely cut in April 1988. Meanwhile, in other areas, local authorities have been invited or required to take on additional responsibilities. For example, it was originally intended that local authority staff should be closely involved in decisions on social fund claims.[19] Under the Social Security Act 1988 local authorities have been given power to make emergency social security payments on behalf of the Secretary of State; and the Children's Bill (1989) allows them to make cash payments for young people.

Within the housing benefit scheme, some discretionary powers have been left in place, while the subsidy system has been altered to ensure that the beneficial use of discretion is prohibitively expensive. In these instances local authorities are left with formal responsibility, and given the legal powers necessary to meet needs; but in most cases they will not have the financial capacity to do so. From central government's point of view, the outright removal of entitlement can have the disadvantage that the failure to meet need becomes a ministerial responsibility. By contrast, the failure of the local authority to meet need when it has powers to do so is likely to be seen locally as the fault of the authority. Arguments about the unfairness or inadequacy of central government subsidy and grant arrangements are highly technical, and can often be countered by allegations of local authority mismanagement or misuse of resources.

Conclusion

Overall, claimants have derived limited benefit from the enhanced role of local authorities in social security provision. Although many local authorities have been keen to use their discretionary powers favourably, central government has been increasingly willing to step in and curtail these powers. Meanwhile, areas of local authority responsibility seem to have been a favoured target for central government spending cuts, even when — as is the case with housing benefit — expenditure has grown in large part as a result of government policies.

The history of housing benefit illustrates very clearly the difficulty of using a means-tested benefit to offset the effects of reductions in housing investment and rises in rents. As the role of housing benefit has become stretched it has become vulnerable to cuts. The government argues that a means-tested benefit aimed at the poor should not involve such huge amounts of expenditure. Yet the obvious conclusion — that the switch away from the direct provision of subsidised housing is placing an unsupportable burden on housing benefit — has not been drawn. Instead it is suggested that housing benefit must be too generous.

The recent experience of housing benefit bodes ill for the poll tax rebates. Expenditure on poll tax rebates is set to rise higher than current spending on rate rebates (see Chapter 2), this time because of the increases in the number of payers and in the level of payments for some poorer households. In order to ease the introduction of the poll tax, the government is also making the rebates scheme more generous for some groups. But there must be a real risk that the government will once again argue that rebates are costing too much; that they are not targeted sufficiently on the poor; and that cuts are necessary.

We have seen that local authorities play a vital role in providing services which form an essential part of the welfare state. These are of especial importance to low-income households who do not have the luxury of being able to turn to the private sector, and whose living standards are much more dependent on public services. Here the concern is that the regressive nature of the poll tax, in conjunction with new constraints on other sources of revenue, will place the funding of local services in jeopardy.

Notes

1 *The Local Right: enabling not providing*, by Nicholas Ridley, Centre for Policy Studies, London, 1988.

2 Responsibility for expenditure here refers to the administration of services or benefits. A considerable proportion of local authority welfare spending is funded by central government grant. In the case of housing benefit, local authorities are to a considerable extent acting as agents administering a central government scheme. Prior to the introduction of housing benefit in 1982/83, local authorities were already responsible for administering rent and rate rebates for those who were on low incomes but not receiving supplementary benefit. Recipients of supplementary benefit were paid an allowance for housing costs which was included in the supplementary benefit payment from the Department of Health and Social Security (as it was then called). After housing benefit was fully introduced in April 1983, local authorities became responsible for the payment of rebates and allowances to all those entitled — whether or not they received supplementary benefit. This arrangement has continued with the replacement of supplementary benefit by income support. Although this represents a significant shift of responsibility to local authorities, it is important to recognise that the rules of entitlement for housing benefit are laid down in Department of Social Security regulations, leaving limited scope for local discretion.

3 Source: *The Government's Expenditure Plans*, 1982/3 to 1984/5, Cmnd 8494, and 1988-9 to 1990-91, Cmnd 288.

4 *Economic Trends*, no 422, December 1988, Central Statistical Office. In order to assess the relative importance of welfare services and cash benefits to different income groups, the CSO attributes a nominal cash value to 'benefits in kind'. The use of services by particular households is estimated on the basis of indicators such as the number of children in the household, and their housing tenure. The most recent such exercise was carried out using the *Family Expenditure Survey 1986* — a government survey of some 7,200 households.

5 *Economic Trends*, no 422, December 1988, Central Statistical Office, Table L.

6 G Bramley, J Le Grand & William Low, 'How far is the poll tax a "community charge"? The implications of service usage evidence'. Discussion paper, Welfare State Programme, ST/ICERD, London School of Economics, April 1989.

7 The survey is based on the use individuals make of the county's services and expenditure is allocated on the basis of their use of those services.

8 *Charity Trends*, 11th Edition, Charities Aid Foundation 1988.

9 *Social Security Statistics, 1988*, HMSO 1988. (Figures rounded to the nearest 10,000.)

10 *Public Finance and Accountancy*, 4 December 1987.

11 See note 7.

12 The rates are also regressive, so the same dilemma arises — but less acutely. Although better-off ratepayers contribute less (in proportion to income) to local services than poorer ratepayers, they contribute considerably more in rates than they will in poll tax.

13 Central government pays a subsidy to local authorities for nearly all the payment and part of the administration of housing benefit.

14 Local schemes applied to claimants of 'standard housing benefit' — ie, those

not on supplementary benefit; the £10 limit on expenditure was also calculated by reference to this element of the scheme.

15 Local authorities can now only spend up to a maximum of 0.1 per cent of their housing benefit expenditure on these discretionary payments.
16 Schedule 3, The Rent Officers (Additional Functions) Order 1989.
17 Press release from DHSS, Dr Boyson's statement, 6 January 1984.
18 Green Paper, *Reform of Social Security*, Cmnd 9517, vol 1, HMSO 1985.
19 See *Reform of Social Security — Programme for Change*, Green Paper, June 1985, Cmnd 9518, vol 2, para 2107; and *Social Fund — Position statement and practice guide*, Association of County Councils and Association of Metropolitan Authorities, January 1988.

2 A guide to the legislation

The recent changes in social security and local government finance are contained principally in three pieces of legislation: the Social Security Act 1986; the Local Government Finance Act 1988 (which applies to England and Wales); and, in Scotland, the reform of local government finance was enacted in the Abolition of Domestic Rates (Scotland) Act 1987. We describe them in some detail below.[1]

Social security reforms

The Social Security Act 1986, most of whose provisions were implemented in April 1988, was described by the government as bringing about the most significant overhaul of benefits since 1948. Its explicit aims were to 'target' resources on those most in need; to simplify benefits; and to make the social security system consistent with the government's economic objectives. The last objective was seen as entailing measures to reduce the proportion of public spending devoted to the social security budget, to encourage work incentives and to increase private provision.

The reforms focused almost entirely on the means-tested part of the social security system. However, some changes did affect the national insurance scheme. For example, major cuts were made to the State Earnings Related Pension Scheme, whose effect will not be felt until the next century; substantial reductions in entitlement to widows' benefits were introduced; and the universal maternity and death grants were abolished in April 1987.

Supplementary benefit was replaced by 'income support'. The weekly additions for special needs such as heating, diet and laundry, which formed part of supplementary benefit, were also scrapped. Instead, the basic rate of income support can now be topped up with premiums based on status such as old age, parenthood, single parenthood, or disability. Additional payments for water rates were also abolished. The single payments scheme, which gave legal entitlement to one-off grants for specific needs such as bedding, furniture, baby items, cookers and household equipment, was replaced by the social fund. Most payments from the social fund come in the form of loans rather than grants. Social fund decisions are discretionary and there is no right of appeal to an independent tribunal. Indeed, the fund is cash-limited, which means that if the money runs out no more payments can be made.

The structure of basic rates was also changed. The higher rate of benefit payable to single householders (those who had set up home on their own), in recognition of the extra costs involved in living independently, was abolished. Instead, a single person (without children) under the age of 25 receives a lower rate of benefit — just £27.40 a week for all living expenses, including bills such as for fuel and water rates; this compares with a weekly rate of £34.90 payable to a single person over 25. Subsequently (in the Social Security Act 1988), the government abolished entitlement to income support for 16- and 17-year-olds altogether, allowing only some very limited exceptions.

Also as part of the April 1988 changes, family credit, a means-tested benefit for families in low-paid work, replaced family income supplement. In its structure, family credit is a more generous benefit, and ministers argued that it would prove to be so in practice. They believed, wrongly (at least to date), that the rate of take-up would be higher for family credit. At the same time, although no change to child benefit was included within the legislation, the Green Paper made it clear that family credit would be prioritised above child benefit in the allocation of extra resources; and that consideration would be given to diverting resources from child benefit to family credit.[2] In practice, the price of the more costly family credit has been a freeze in child benefit. The free school meals service was also cut back: family credit claimants no longer qualify for free school meals, and the power of local authorities to offer free school meals to other families on low incomes was removed. Free school meals are now confined to children in families on income support. Again the justification was that notional cash compensation for the loss of free school meals in the family credit structure would compensate poorer families.

The structure of means-tested benefits was harmonised so that entitlement to each is now calculated according to similar rules. In particular, both housing benefit and family credit are now assessed on the basis of net income (after payment of tax and national insurance), in line with income support. Moreover, for the most part the basic rates for income support also form the basis of the housing benefit calculation. This means that 18- to 24-year-olds not only receive less income support than their older counterparts; but if they are in work or on a training scheme and live independently they also receive less housing benefit. Moreover, their entitlement to poll tax rebates will be reduced for the same reason.

Along with the harmonisation of structure came massive cuts in housing benefit — well over £600 million in the first year according to government estimates (see Chapter 1, table 1.3). Most significantly for our purposes, the maximum rate rebate was reduced from 100 to 80 per cent: so, whereas supplementary benefit claimants did not have to pay rates, those on income support must pay one-fifth of the full amount. (A compensatory adjustment was made to income support levels — this is discussed in detail below). The arguments for this change related to the accountability of local government rather than the needs of claimants, and the new rule is being carried forward to apply to the poll tax. In Chapter 4 we examine the government's case for this measure in detail and look at the way it has worked in practice during its first year of operation.

Other changes to housing benefit were also very significant. 'Tapers' govern the rate at which rebates are withdrawn as income rises. These were increased sharply, with the result that housing benefit is lost at much lower levels of income. Indeed for every extra £1 of net income over the taper, the claimant now loses 65 pence of their rent rebate and 20 pence of their rate rebate. As we discussed in Chapter 1, the discretionary power of local authorities to run 'local schemes', paying extra housing benefit to groups of claimants, was abolished.

Bringing in the poll tax

The government announced its intention of introducing a poll tax to replace rates, in a Green Paper published in January 1986.[3] Legislation was first introduced for Scotland (The Abolition of Domestic Rates Etc (Scotland) Act 1987), and subsequently for England and Wales (The Local Government Finance Act 1988). The poll tax is not being introduced in Northern Ireland. The first poll tax bills in Scotland were due for payment in April 1989. In England and Wales the process of registering people for the poll tax takes place over the summer and autumn of 1989. Payment starts in April 1990.

The poll tax is a flat-rate tax which varies from one district council area to another.[4] It is set so as to provide sufficient revenue to fund the services of all the authorities which provide services in the area. For example, in Scotland this would include spending by the regional and district councils;[5] in English rural districts it would include the expenditure of the county and district council. Unlike rates, which are effectively a tax on households, the poll tax is a tax on each individual: every adult (over the age of 18) is liable for the tax, unless they fall into one of the few exempt categories. Indeed, the poll tax will vastly extend the net of taxation: in England alone, the number of people liable for local taxes will almost double from approximately 18 million to around 36 million.

Types of poll tax and exemptions

There are three sorts of poll tax. The **personal community charge** is the ordinary poll tax payable by almost all adults over age 18 who are solely or mainly resident in an area. Where someone lives in an area for part of the year only, liability is assessed on a daily basis, so s/he has to pay a proportion of the annual poll tax in that area. The **standard community charge** is payable by the owner of a house or flat where no one is liable for the personal community charge. Long-term lease-holders are also liable for the standard charge. The **collective community charge** is levied on properties such as short-stay hostels. Landlords of these properties must pay the collective community charge on behalf of the residents, who in turn are liable to make 'contributions' to the landlord equivalent to a daily personal community charge.

Certain groups are exempt from the poll tax altogether — although the categories are defined very restrictively. The exempt groups are: prisoners (whether on remand or convicted, but not including those jailed for non-payment of the poll tax or of a poll tax fine); diplomatic agents and some foreign military personnel; people who are 'severely mentally impaired' (that is, severely mentally handicapped as the result of a congenital disease or accident); 18-year-olds for whom child benefit is still payable; monks and nuns; people who are resident in hospital, a home or a hostel and who receive care or treatment there; volunteer residential care workers; some residents of Crown buildings; some people staying in short-stay charitable hostels or night shelters; and people of no fixed abode. In addition, full-time students only have to pay 20 per cent of their poll tax bills.

Rebates

The poll tax rebate scheme, or what the government calls the 'community charge benefit', is closely modelled on the rate rebate component of housing benefit, in the form it has taken since the April 1988 cuts. Although the poll tax is a tax on individuals, poll tax rebates are to be assessed on a family basis. In the case of couples, the poll tax liability is treated as twice that payable by an individual; any income received by either partner is counted in the assessment. If a rebate is due, entitlement is divided equally between the two partners.

The maximum rebate payable is 80 per cent — so that everyone has to pay at least one-fifth of the poll tax, irrespective of income.[6] The maximum rebate is payable if the claimant is on income support or if their income falls below income support level. For example, a pensioner couple cease to be entitled to income support if their joint net weekly income exceeds £71.85, while the threshold for a single person aged under 25 is £27.40 (1989/90 benefit rates). If the claimant's assessed income is below these thresholds then normally 80 per cent of the poll tax is rebated.[7]

If the assessed income exceeds these thresholds, then part or all of the rebate will be withdrawn. The claimant loses 15 pence in rebate for each additional £1 above their threshold. This is more generous than the rate rebate scheme after the April 1988 cuts, where the 'taper' is 20 pence in the pound. Nevertheless, the poll tax rebate entitlement quickly tapers away to zero. Moreover, no rebate is payable if the calculated weekly entitlement falls below a 'minimum amount', currently set at 50 pence. If the claimant has more than £3,000 in savings, they are assessed as receiving notional income. In practice, this means that 15 pence of the rebate is lost for each additional £250 of capital. However, if savings exceed £8,000 there is no entitlement to rebate at all.

There is no right of appeal to an independent tribunal against decisions relating to 'community charge benefit'. As with housing benefit, a claimant can apply for a decision to be considered by a review board consisting of councillors from the same authority which made the initial decision.

Table 2.1 Caseload and costs of the poll tax rebate scheme — latest estimates

	Poll tax rebates			Rate rebates	
	caseload thousands	(individuals) thousands	cost £ million	caseload thousands	cost £ million
England	6,860	(9,380)	1,525	5,115	1,265
Scotland	780	(1,040)	165	600	160
Wales	440	(600)	60	295	45
Great Britain	8,080	(11,020)	1,750	6,015	1,470

Source: *House of Commons Hansard*, 19 October 1988, col 898.

1 The caseload figures in columns one and four are take-up estimates of numbers of claimants. They thus treat both partners in a married or unmarried couple as one. Column two gives the estimated number of individuals who would receive a poll tax rebate.

2 The rate rebate figures are estimates for 1988-89.

3 The poll tax rebate figures are based on a maximum benefit of 80 per cent of liability and a prescribed taper of 15 per cent. The current housing benefit rules for assessing the levels of the applicable amounts, the treatment of capital and income and a minimum benefit of 50p per week per claim have been used throughout. The figures are based on the most recent illustrative estimates of what poll taxes would have been in 1988-89 had they been in operation.

Note: It is important to note that the comparison on which this table is based is between spending on poll tax rebates and spending on rate rebates *after* the April 1988 cuts: for example, the figures assume that claimants are already paying 20 per cent of their rates, and so they do not reflect the effect of the 1988 cut to rebate entitlement.

The huge increase in the number of local taxpayers, allied to the more generous taper, means a substantial increase in the number of rebate recipients (by around one-third to some 8 million) and in the cost of rebates (by an estimated £280 million) (see table 2.1).[8]

Compensation for 20 per cent payments

Shortly before the general election in 1987, the Secretary of State for Social Services announced that some compensation would be included within income support for the 20 per cent contribution which claimants would have to start making from April 1988. This principle is being carried forward to apply to the 20 per cent poll tax contribution as well.

However, this undertaking was of less value than might at first appear. Firstly, the compensation has been based on a 'guesstimate' of average poll tax levels payable by claimants. It has been provided for by a once-off adjustment to income support rates in April 1989 — announced before the Scottish poll tax levels were known, and some 18 months before the poll tax is payable south of the border. We now know that government projections of poll tax levels in Scotland fell substantially short of the actual figures (see Chapter 9). Moreover, because the compensatory element is not a separate allowance, in future it will simply be uprated by the same amount as the rest of income support; this may or may not keep pace with actual poll tax levels.

Secondly, the compensation is based on an *average* poll tax that claimants have to pay. This is of benefit to claimants who live in areas with below average poll taxes, but leaves others with a shortfall which they must make up by using money which is intended for other essential living expenses such as food, clothing and heating.

Finally, the promise to 'add' compensation for poll tax payments on to income support was of limited value because the government did not fully uprate the illustrative income support rates (which had been announced in the White Paper) in line with inflation.[9] The result was a cut of 50 pence per week for a single person and £1 for a couple. This was carried forward to the April 1989 rates of income support and there are no plans to restore it.

The register

Each authority responsible for collecting the poll tax has a Community Charge Registration Officer (CCRO).[10] CCROs have substantial powers in their own right to draw up the register, requiring information from both individuals and their own authorities. So in law elected members have very limited influence over the registration process.

The register shows the individual's name and address — and the address in respect of which the poll tax is being levied if this is different (for standard and collective poll tax). Individuals on the register are supposed to be sent a copy of their entry, and they have a right of appeal if they believe they are wrongly entered as liable. A summary of the register is available for public inspection.

Individuals are obliged to provide to the CCRO the information about themselves on which the register is based. In addition, they can be treated as responsible for providing information about other adults living in a particular property: for example, a tenant may be obliged to fill out a form for all the adults living in the flat or house; and a social worker responsible for supportive accommodation, such as a house for ex-psychiatric patients, may have to register the adults living there. Failure to provide information which is required under the law can lead to the imposition by the CCRO of a 'civil penalty' of £50, followed by further penalties of £200 for each subsequent offence.

The CCRO is also legally entitled to gain access to a wide range of official information. S/he can check the poll tax register against the electoral register. S/he can require the local authority to hand over the names and addresses of individuals who have claimed housing benefit, who have a social worker, or who have consulted an advice centre. The Secretary of State for Social Security is empowered to hand over names and addresses of income support claimants to CCROs.

Joint and several liability

Although the tax is supposed to be a tax on individuals, the Green Paper recognised that in practice many individuals do not have enough money of their own with which to pay such a bill:

> In principle, each individual should ... be liable for paying his or her bill. However, this might be difficult where people have no independent income of their own.[11]

The solution adopted in the legislation is to treat men and women who are married or cohabiting as 'jointly and severally liable' for the poll tax.

This means that either partner can be held liable for the total amount owed by the couple. The rule can be applied retrospectively, so that where a relationship has broken down a ruling of joint and several liability could mean one partner having to pay for debts incurred by the other partner during the period of the relationship.

The respective incomes of the two partners during the period when the debt arose are irrelevant to a determination of joint and several liability.

In the case of a man and a woman who are not married but live together, the authority determines joint and several liability using the same criteria as for the cohabitation rule in social security. These include: the existence of a sexual relationship; the arrangement of private finances; whether or not the two people have had children together; and 'public acknowledgement' (for example whether neighbours perceive the two people as a married couple).

In theory, the need to decide whether joint and several liability applies only arises when someone falls into arrears. So the CCRO does not have powers to demand information regarding marriage status or cohabitation, beyond the names and addresses of liable individuals. Nevertheless, more than one CCRO has requested information on the registration form about the personal relationships between adults in each household. There may be nothing unlawful about requesting such information on a voluntary basis, although it would be wrong (and possibly unlawful) for the registration officer to imply that individuals are in any way obliged to respond.

Collection and enforcement

Everyone agrees that the poll tax is considerably more expensive to collect than the rates. The government commissioned the accountants, Price Waterhouse, to estimate the extra costs in England. Price Waterhouse calculated the setting-up costs in 1989/90 to be £244-287 million and estimated the annual running costs at £379-435 million, compared with a figure of approximately £200 million spent collecting the rates. The local authority associations carried out a more comprehensive survey and estimated the annual running costs to be £495 million.[12]

For many people the poll tax will entail a different method of payment from the rates. Rates are often paid with rents as part of an inclusive charge: for example, this arrangement is the norm for council tenants. However, since the poll tax is an individual tax, it will generally have to be paid separately from rents. Individuals will normally be entitled to pay by monthly instalments.[13] More frequent instalments may be offered at the discretion of local authorities.

Once an individual (or their partner) falls into arrears, there are a number of enforcement procedures available to local authorities. Authorities must first apply to the magistrates' court (England and Wales) for a liability order; in Scotland, the application is to the Sheriff, who need not hold a hearing, for a summary warrant. The liability order specifies the amount of poll tax owed, plus costs. The

Scottish summary warrant is similar, but a 10 per cent surcharge is automatically added to the bill.

Authorities can then apply to have the money owing deducted from a claimant's income support. If the debtor is in work, they can order the employer to deduct payments from earnings. In addition, the debtor's personal possessions can be seized and sold off.[14] The authority may also recover the debt by freezing assets held by the debtor, for instance in a bank account. In England and Wales, if the authority fails to recover the amount owed by seizure of personal possessions, it can go back to the magistrates' court and apply to have the debtor imprisoned. This is imprisonment for a civil debt and does not imply that non-payment is a criminal offence. In Scotland, imprisonment is not allowed.

The new financial system

The switch from a property tax to a flat-rate tax on individuals changes the distribution of the tax burden between rich and poor, and between different types of households. But it does not directly affect the amount of revenue which each local authority has to raise to finance its services, other than by increasing the costs of collection. However, changes being introduced at the same time as the poll tax do substantially affect the revenue which each authority has to raise through domestic taxes. (By domestic taxes we mean those taxes paid by individuals and households, as opposed to non-domestic taxes paid by businesses.) In turn this will mean that in many areas the average tax bill per household will change dramatically. These changes to the system of local government finance are discussed in more detail in Chapter 8.

There are two main changes. Firstly, the business rate is changing significantly. In England and Wales, the local business rate is being abolished altogether from 1990. Instead, there will be a national non-domestic rate, with the level set by central government. This means that local authorities will no longer have any power to vary their income from the business rate. Local authorities will act as collection agents for central government. The proceeds will be redistributed to local authorities in proportion to their adult population. In Scotland, income from the business rate continues for the time being to be retained by the authority which collects it, but the amount charged is limited by government order. The Secretary of State for Scotland has announced that he will take further powers to limit the amount charged by individual authorities, so that over a period of five years the Scottish business rate will be integrated into the national system.[15]

The second major change is to the grant system. Rates pay for less than half of local authority spending; the rest comes from central government grant. Previously, these grants varied according to the expenditure of the authority. Under the new system, every authority receives the same grant irrespective of local spending decisions. Major changes are also being made to the formula which determines the distribution of grant, which will cause a substantial shift in grant entitlement between authorities (see Chapter 8). These and other alterations to the financial system entail huge changes in the amount of revenue which particular local authorities have to raise from domestic taxpayers. For example, the amount which authorities serving Richmond (in Yorskhire) have to raise from local taxpayers is projected to increase from around £6 million to £7.9 million, an increase of over 30 per cent.[16]

However, the changes are to be phased in by a system of 'safety nets'. These provide authorities which stand to lose from the changes with a temporary increase in grant, funded by reductions in the grant entitlement of authorities which gain from the changes. Safety nets mean that, in the first year of the poll tax, changes to the financial system will have little impact on the average tax bill in each authority area. But, as safety nets are phased out, the effects of the new financial system will be felt more and more strongly on the average bill in each area. In England and Wales, safety nets are to be phased out over four years, so that 1994/95 will be the first year in which the new financial arrangements are fully implemented. In Scotland, the position is less certain: safety nets are to be phased out over three to five years.

The new system will have an immediate impact by narrowing the revenue base on which local authorities can rely when determining the local level of taxation. The nationalisation of the business rate, and the transitional arrangements applying to it in Scotland, mean that the only source of revenue for additional spending is the poll tax. The government argues that this provides a clear link between taxation and spending: each additional £1 of spending per adult results in another £1 on the poll tax. However, the poll tax provides only a small proportion of local authority revenue (approximately one-quarter). Therefore, on average, a 5 per cent increase in spending on services would require a disproportionate increase of around 20 per cent in the poll tax. We return to a more detailed analysis of this question — known as the problem of 'gearing' — in Chapter 9.

Conclusion

The social security changes implemented in April 1988 concentrated on means-tested benefits. The relationship between the different means-tested benefits has been harmonised up to a point, but there have been substantial cuts to housing benefit — particularly the introduction of a maximum rebate for rates (or the poll tax) of 80 per cent. Discretion has been given a crucial role in the form of the social fund, which is cash-limited, has no independent appeal procedure, and for the most part offers payments in the form of loans, not grants.

The flat-rate poll tax is levied on nearly every adult at a level set by local authorities in each area. Local authorities have considerable powers with which to enforce payment of the poll tax. A new financial system is being introduced for local government alongside the poll tax — incorporating the nationalisation of the business rate and the complete revision of the grant system.

Notes

1   A short guide to the poll tax is also available (free) from LGIU: *Ability to Pay* (by Peter Esam, Geoff Fimister and Carey Oppenheim, LGIU, AMA and CPAG, April 1989). It explains the government's proposals for poll tax rebates. The Scottish poll tax is explained in the *Poll Tax Handbook* (Scottish TUC, Scottish Council for Civil Liberties and Scottish LGIU, February 1989).
2   *Reform of Social Security — Programme for Change*, Green Paper, June 1985, Cmnd 9518, Vol 2, para 4.49.
3   *Paying for Local Government*, HMSO, January 1986, Cmnd 9714.
4   The term 'district council area' is used here as a general term to include areas such as non-metropolitan (shire) districts, metropolitan districts, London boroughs and Scottish island councils.
5   However, the island councils are single-tier authorities.
6   Obviously the 20 per cent 'minimum payment' does not apply to exempt individuals, who pay nothing.
7   'Assessed income' here is net of tax and national insurance. 'Disregards' are allowed against earned income — eg, the first £10 pw of a couple's earned income is ignored. Notional income is assumed on any savings over £3,000.
8   Another factor is that there will be no deduction from poll tax rebates in respect of an assumed contribution from 'non-dependants' living in the household: instead they will be liable for their own poll tax.
9   *Reform of Social Security*, Technical Annexe, Cmnd 9691, 1985.
10   In Scotland this is the Electoral Registration Officer and Regional Assessor, and in England and Wales it is the Chief Finance Officer of the authority. Also in Scotland, the regional councils are responsible for collecting the poll tax. In England and Wales it is collected by the district councils (or metropolitan districts/London boroughs).
11   *Paying for Local Government*, HMSO, Cmnd 9714, para G.27, 1986.
12   *Public Finance and Accountancy*, 1 July 1988.
13   There will be ten monthly instalments in England and Wales, 12 in Scotland.
14   In Scotland this is known as 'poinding' goods for a warrant sale; certain essential goods cannot be seized. In England and Wales the process is known as 'levying distress', or 'distraint'.
15   The government plans to incorporate Scotland into the national business rate system over a number of years, by gradually bringing the poundage charged by individual Scottish authorities into line with the uniform figure for England and Wales.
16   These figures are based on 1988/89 prices and local expenditure levels. See Chapter 6 for details of our calculations and sources.

3 The government's objectives – an exposition

We have a different vision of what it means to 'protect and promote economic and social welfare' in this country. We believe that dependence in the long run decreases human happiness and reduces human freedom. We believe the well-being of individuals is best protected and promoted when they are helped to be independent, to use their talents to take care of themselves and their families, and to achieve things on their own, which is one of the greatest satisfactions life can offer.

(Speech by Rt Hon John Moore MP, Secretary of State for Social Security, 26 September 1987)

The community charge certainly is fairer than domestic rates, but it scores far higher on a number of other counts. Morality, in this context, includes fairness, but it also encompasses responsibility and self-reliance — the idea that local authorities should be responsible to all of their electors, that every adult should pay his fair share and play a responsible part in the local democratic process. Morality is concerned not only with helping people who have difficulty helping themselves, but also with giving them the means to stand on their own two feet.

(Speech by Rt Hon John Selwyn Gummer MP, Minister of State for Local Government, at Blakeney, Norfolk, 7 October 1988)

The themes which the government calls upon in defence of its recent social security policies and of the poll tax are linked. One part of the government's stance is essentially defensive. It attempts to counter criticisms that its policies have been unfair and regressive. It argues that, on the contrary, help is now better targeted on those most in need; and that means-tested benefits protect the poor from losses, whether due to the flat-rate poll tax, or to rising costs such as increased rents, or the erosion of universal entitlements such as child benefit.

But another part of the government's case is more positive in character. The government argues that its policies empower individuals in relation to the state. In the case of social security, reforms are said to have reduced dependency on state welfare, and promoted self-reliance. The poll tax, meanwhile, is advocated on the basis that it increases the accountability of local government to the voters, and will extend personal choice. In this chapter, we lay out the government's case in more detail without attempting to assess its strengths and weaknesses.

Breaking free of state welfare?

The concern that the provision of state welfare may increase dependency and reduce self-reliance is not a new one. But since the introduction of the Beveridge reforms after the war, it has usually focused on the worry that means-tested benefits demean their recipients; and that the growing reliance on these benefits undermines the notion of entitlement on which universal benefits are based. Thus, in 1974, when she was Secretary of State for Social Services, Barbara Castle made the following statement:

> An income adequate to live on must become the prerogative of every family, but the ways in which we make that income available are just as important as the money itself. Today too much of our welfare system tends to pauperise. In future every step we take must be designed to build self-respect. This means we must not separate the poor from the rest of society by ... doling out means-tested supplements to inadequate wages or insurance benefits.[1]

However, the Conservative government of the 1980s has rejected this approach. The view that national insurance should be strengthened in order to eliminate reliance on means-tested benefits is dismissed as irrelevant to the central question — the relationship between state provision and the provision individuals 'make for themselves' through the private sector (including occupational provision) and self-help.[2] This relationship was defined in the 1985 Green Paper in terms of a partnership — but a partnership in which the state's role is confined to meeting needs in ways which do not interfere with the expression of self-reliance and individual responsibility:

> State provision has an important role in supporting and sustaining the individual; but it should not discourage self-reliance or stand in the way of individual provision and responsibility.[3]

So the government's conceptual framework is one in which state benefits are necessary to provide for those in need, but the self-reliant and responsible individual is able to make provision for her or his own needs 'privately'.

This approach was seen most explicitly in the changes made to pensions under the Social Security Act 1986. These measures offered the opportunity and financial incentive for individuals to opt out of the State Earnings Related Pension Scheme (SERPS) (or out of an occupational scheme), in order to take out a personal pension. At the same time, future entitlements under SERPS were severely cut. The government's approach was subsequently defended by the Secretary of State for Social Security:

> Here again our aim is to allow personal initiative and effort to flourish unhindered by the state... A well-ordered market responding to the forces of demand and competition and which enables individuals to select the type of pension that suits them best, is an important and visible symbol of our overall philosophy.[4]

Targeting

The government has repeatedly argued that restricting public expenditure on social security can be reconciled with protecting the poor; indeed, that the poor can be provided with *additional* help. The notion used to square the circle is 'targeting': the idea that extra help can be focused on the poorest claimants through means-tested benefits, while benefits for others are restricted or curtailed. It is in these terms that the government's decision to freeze child benefit for two years has been defended by ministers. On 1 March 1988, John Moore MP made the following comment in a letter to MPs:

> By focusing help more precisely on priority groups, particularly low-income families with children, we will ensure better targeting of resources, thus we will be spending over £200 million extra on low-income working families through family credit...[5]

Indeed, family credit was described by Norman Fowler (then Secretary of State for Social Services) as the 'flagship' of the government's reforms, epitomising the advantages of targeting. In contrast to the universal child benefit, family credit would only go to those most in need.

This emphasis on targeting through means-tested benefits has an important indirect link with the encouragement of private provision. Means-tested benefits are seen as better adapted than universal ones to the proper role of state welfare — to meet those needs for which private provision is unavailable:

> Our measures are designed to strengthen the *proper* role of the state by ensuring that resources go more clearly and are more fairly given to those who need them most.[6] (*our emphasis*)

Targeting is also seen as the best way to protect the poorest from policies which either extend the principle of charging or seek to bring charges up to market levels, whether in the field of school meals, rents, or local authority services. Thus it is the task of means-tested benefits to protect the poor from the risks which follow from extending the market principle in local authority finance.

In the case of the poll tax, the government has sought to counter criticisms of the regressive nature of the tax by introducing a rebate scheme slightly better than the rate rebate scheme which emerged from the April 1988 cuts. Originally this improvement formed no part of the government's plans but, under pressure from a rebellion organised by Michael Mates MP before the Report stage of the Local Government Finance Bill, a concession was announced: the rate at which poll tax rebates would be withdrawn (the 'taper') would be set at 15 pence in the pound rather than 20 pence (see Chapter 2). Following this announcement, the Rt Hon Nicholas Ridley MP, Secretary of State for the Environment, said:

> We have made our rebate system more generous, but we have targeted it very much better... I can think of no scheme more closely attuned to ability to pay.[7]

Just as, in relation to recent social security cuts, targeting has been held out as offering protection for the poor, here it is proposed that they can be protected from a flat-rate tax in the same way.

In summary, the government's approach is to reduce the role of state social security and encourage private provision instead, in the belief that state support necessarily entails dependence, whereas private welfare is identified with self-reliance and independence. Where state support is necessary — and it is acknowledged that some state social security provision is essential — then it is preferable that its role should be limited. This objective, it is argued, can be achieved by targeting resources on those most in need through means-testing. Moreover, this approach is supposed to provide protection for the poor while market disciplines are imposed on local public services. The hope is that in these ways a natural inclination of individuals to provide for themselves through private welfare will — for most people most of the time — supplant the necessity for state provision.

Local services and personal choice

The government's arguments in favour of introducing the poll tax also reflect these themes of independence and self-reliance. The new local government finance system forms part of an extensive package of reforms intended to bring about a new relationship between the individual, private provision and local government. Recent legislation has enabled schools to opt out of local education authority control, and housing estates to be taken over by private landlords. Local authorities are also being compelled to put contracts for major services such as street cleaning out to tender, so that private firms can take over from directly employed staff. The Environment Minister,

Michael Howard MP, summed up the government's hopes for these changes as follows:

> More choice for tenants. More involvement for parents. And now more power for local voters. All our policies are designed to give people more control over their own lives.[8]

Again, one element of the government's argument is that responsibility and choice are enhanced if state provision is limited to its proper role of providing for those most in need. Lord Caithness has spelled out the application of this philosophy to the government's housing policies:

> We believe that people can, should and want to take responsibility for their housing. The market should meet the needs of the great majority of the population, responding to their choices. State resources should be concentrated on those people who are genuinely not able to compete in the market. And they too should have far more choice than they have in the past, including the right to change their landlord if they do not get a decent service.[9]

Thus the provision of local government services is seen as inhibiting personal freedom. The government believes that the financial discipline imposed by the poll tax and the new system of finance will curb over-powerful local authorities, and in the process give greater responsibility and control to individuals.

Accountability

The government's arguments for the poll tax focus to a great extent on the promotion of accountability. It believes that local government's accountability to voters rests on the principle that everyone who votes should contribute to the cost of local services through local taxation. The poll tax is intended to achieve this goal in combination with the cut in the maximum rebate payable from 100 per cent to 80 per cent (see Chapter 2). Nicholas Ridley, the Secretary of State for the Environment, put the argument as follows:

> Everyone should have the right, through the ballot box, to influence the level of service that is provided and the price that they must pay through their taxes. That is the essence of accountability and of responsible democratic control of the services provided by local authorities.[10]

To some extent the financial discipline involved in this notion of local accountability applies more directly to voters than to local authorities themselves. The relationship is seen as reciprocal: the individual exercises control through the ballot box and must therefore also pay, through taxation. Indeed, ministers have repeatedly said that one of their main objections to the rates is that a large number of people have the vote without being individually liable for local taxation:

> We have a system in which control of local government's £45 million gross annual spending is vested in 35 million electors. Yet only 18 million are liable to pay rates and more than 3 million of those receive a full rebate. The fact is that 20 million of the local electorate make no direct contribution to the cost of local services.[11]

Thus the introduction of 20 per cent contributions to local taxation by income support claimants formed part of a process of ensuring that what electors vote for they also pay for.

The poll tax applies this principle in other ways as well. As a tax on individuals, the spouses of householders, as well as non-householders, have to pay it. (A non-householder is an adult who shares accommodation, but who does not have responsibility for meeting housing costs: for example, a young person living with her parents.) Moreover, the abolition of the local business rate, along with the changes to the grant system (see Chapter 8), mean that for many services the poll tax is the *only* source of revenue which varies to take account of changes to expenditure. Thus any extra spending which is not financed by charges such as rents falls entirely on domestic taxpayers.

In the government's view these measures present local voters with a clearer choice about the optimum level of spending by their local council. Each voter is supposed to have a clear interest in the outcome of local spending decisions, because she or he will contribute directly to the financing of those decisions. Moreover, it is suggested that the relationship between spending decisions and levels of local taxation is more simple and direct under the poll tax than under the old system.

Individual power

It may not be immediately apparent what this notion of an extended financial discipline has to do with individual freedom and responsibility. To some extent, the government equates a *clearer* choice with *more* choice. Thus, as we saw above, Michael Howard MP has suggested that the poll tax implies 'more power for local voters'. There is also an image of the 'responsible individual', best encapsulated by John Selwyn Gummer MP's quotation at the start of this chapter: '...every adult should pay his fair share and play a responsible part in the local democratic process'. Whereas in relation to social security the responsible and self-reliant person is seen as an individual free of contact with the state, here responsibility is seen as entailing a relationship with the state through the payment of taxes.

But there is another element to the government's thinking on the relationship between accountability and personal initiative. Formally the new financial system is presented as promoting greater choice for voters, an argument which envisages the possibility of local spending going up or down, according to the wishes of the electorate. However, the government also believes that in practice local authority provision is likely to shrink as a result of the poll tax, precisely because of the financial discipline it imposes on voters. For example, speaking of the cuts introduced by the new administration in Bradford, Nicholas Ridley MP made it clear that he could not pronounce on detailed aspects of policy. He then went on, referring to the council leader, Eric Pickles:

> But the general philosophy he is pursuing can only be in the interests of the citizens of Bradford, particularly in the community charge era... It is right that if Bradford wants an extravagant council it should pay for it. If it wants a lean council it should get the benefit of a reduced community charge.[12]

In turn, the new breed of 'leaner councils' is seen as allowing greater scope for personal freedom and initiative. The Chancellor summed up the government's overall approach when he spoke — with reference to education and housing policy — of the necessity for central government action with the aim of 'removing the shackles of local government'.[13]

Fairness

Fairness in taxation was treated by the Green Paper which proposed the poll tax as comprising two components: taxation should be related to ability to pay, and should reflect the use made of local services.[14] The Green Paper argued that no local tax could meet both these definitions of fairness, but the poll tax would be no worse than the rates in taking account of ability to pay; and, on the assumption that each adult makes equal use of local services, the poll tax would be closer to a fair charge for these services than the rates.

The government responds to criticisms that the poll tax is unfair by arguing that it is not a tax at all, but rather a 'charge for services' — hence the official name, 'community charge'. They point out that in market transactions people pay for the use they make of services; and that charges are made without respect to income. The principle of charging for particular local services can therefore be extended to incorporate a general charge for the 'bundle of services' which individuals receive from local authorities.

This argument was clearly put forward in the pamphlet widely credited with having convinced the government of the merits of the poll tax, by Douglas Mason. The author describes the poll tax as 'a payment, not a progressive tax', and goes on to explain:

> The principal objective that is made to a per capita tax is that it is regressive, that it involves the least well off paying a higher proportion of their incomes than the wealthy. It is an argument that could be applied to any charge for goods and services. The rich and the poor pay the same to tax their cars, the same for a TV licence, and the same to use a swimming pool or hire a council hall. There seems to be no good reason, therefore, why they should not pay the same for other council services such as refuse collection, police, and fire protection, or the provision and maintenance of roads.[15]

The government's Green Paper made it clear that the arguments for extending the use of charging for particular local government services depend primarily on a preference for the application of market disciplines to service provision. This market-oriented approach is seen as promoting efficiency and personal choice:

> Charging has benefits in terms of efficiency as well as accountability. Where consumers have a choice whether to pay for a service or not, those who provide the service can accurately judge the real level of demand.[16]

Recognising that in practice it is impossible to levy specific charges for many services, the Green Paper argues that a 'community charge' for all services is the next best thing.

Nicholas Ridley MP has also made it clear that the analogy between market disciplines and the financial discipline imposed on voters is intended to be a close one:

> The community charge will be a flat-rate charge for local services. It has to be a flat-rate charge because crucial to the change is the concept that there should be a 'price' for local government services. Like prices for goods in the shops, the community charge 'price' can only work properly if it is roughly the same for everyone.[17]

So the government hopes that the poll tax will bring not only accountability but also choice in that people will be able, in theory, to vote for the level of services they want. Thus the poll tax is seen as introducing a market mechanism into the generality of local government services: individuals will now be able to vote for a level of services that they personally will receive. However, the government has not brought forward proposals to show how this link between individual payment of a tax and individual benefit from service provision can be achieved; nor has it researched the extent to which such a link is achieved at present.

Efficiency

The government argued that its reform of local government finance would meet a further objective, in addition to those of accountability and fairness: 'technical adequacy'. By 'technical adequacy' the government meant that the tax should be reasonably easy to collect and should provide a suitable source of revenue for local government services. The Green Paper argues that the poll tax:

> ...would be capable of producing a yield equivalent to that of rates, would be suitable for all tiers of local government, and would be conducive to proper financial control.[18]

An earlier Green Paper had dismissed the option of introducing a poll tax on the grounds that it would be hard to enforce, would be seen as a tax on the right to vote, and would be both complicated and expensive.[19] The 1986 Green Paper quotes these objections and dismisses them as 'not insuperable'.

Conclusion

The government claims it wishes to enhance individual freedom and responsibility, and sees that objective as entailing a shrinking of government activity. It rejects the view that within the state system universal benefits based on entitlement foster self-respect and dignity, in contrast to means-tested benefits which demean their recipients. Instead, the government argues that the key relationship is the one between provision by the state and by the individual; a reliance on state benefits entails dependency, and the responsible individual is the one who is able to make provision for her or his needs privately.

The aim of the poll tax is to create a new relationship of accountability between individuals and local government. This notion of accountability is closely related to financial discipline: voters are to face the discipline of paying (in taxation) for the level of services which elected representatives choose to provide. The responsible individual is seen as someone able to pay their way by meeting the local tax bill. However, although the poll tax is seen as bringing more choice to voters, the assumption is that it will result in reductions in levels of service provision and that this will free individuals from the 'shackles of local government'.

The government has sought to defend the introduction of a flat-rate tax by playing down the importance of relating local taxation to ability to pay, playing up the 'generosity' of the means-tested rebates scheme and by proposing an alternative definition of fairness — that taxes should relate to the *use* taxpayers make of services. The poll tax is seen as a 'charge', which promises to introduce the benefits of market efficiency and choice to local democracy. Finally, the poll tax is seen as a practicable and workable alternative to rates.

These issues set the agenda for any evaluation of the poll tax and recent social security policies.

Notes

1   'Family life in modern society', a speech by Barbara Castle, 25 October 1974, quoted in *Social Security: the case for reform*, by Ruth Lister, Child Poverty Action Group, 1975.
2   *Reform of Social Security*, Vol 1, para 1.7, HMSO, Cmnd 9517.
3   As note 2.
4   Speech by Rt Hon J Moore MP, 26 September 1987.
5   Rt Hon John Moore MP, letter to MPs, 1 March 1988.
6   As note 4.
7   *House of Commons Hansard*, 18 April 1988, col 588.
8   Michael Howard MP, speech to Conservative National Local Government Conference, 5 March 1988.
9   Lord Caithness, Minister for Housing, speech at the annual lunch of the National House-Building Council, 30 November 1988.
10 Rt Hon Nicholas Ridley MP, *House of Commons Hansard*, 18 April 1988, col 581.
11 As note 10.
12 Rt Hon Nicholas Ridley MP, Secretary of State for the Environment, interviewed by Robert Hedley, *Local Government Chronicle*, 4 November 1988.
13 Rt Hon Nigel Lawson MP, *The New Britain: the tide of ideas from Attlee to Thatcher*, Centre for Policy Studies 1988.
14 *Paying for Local Government*, HMSO, Cmnd 9714, January 1986.
15 Douglas Mason, *Revising the Rating System*, Adam Smith Institute, 1985.
16 *Paying for Local Government*, para 7.4, Cmnd 9714, HMSO, January 1986.
17 Rt Hon Nicholas Ridley MP, Secretary of State for the Environment, speech at Liverpool, 3 August 1987.
18 *Paying for Local Government*, para 3.38, HMSO, Cmnd 9714.
19 *Alternatives to Domestic Rates*, Green Paper, HMSO, Cmnd 8449, 1981.

4 Paying the rates

In April 1988, for the first time, people entitled to subsistence-level benefits had to contribute to their rates. This change was conceived as an extension of accountability. In practice, it worked by intensifying financial discipline on the voters.

The introduction of the 20 per cent contribution to rates — a forerunner to the poll tax — was undertaken for objectives related to local government, not social security. Claimants who received inadequate 'compensation' for the payment have been pushed below the poverty line. It seems to be government policy that this should have been so — even the poorest residents should have to pay for the consequences of living in an area which votes for high spending.

Douglas Mason's pamphlet advocated a poll tax on which many aspects of the government's measures were based (see Chapter 2). In it he argued that losses for claimants in areas with high local taxation were a justifiable consequence of accountability. Claimants should not be spared the just consequences of being part of a community which favoured higher spending. They should be paid a flat-rate allowance to cover an average poll tax contribution, and should have to meet any excess out of their subsistence benefits:

> Those who elected an expensive council committed to costly policies would themselves have to find the extra required, over and above the flat rate, while those who elected a low-spending, low-taxing council would be able to keep the difference and spend it as they chose.[1]

Hardship

Some of the case studies collected by the National Association of Citizens' Advice Bureaux from their local bureaux illustrate the problems that claimants have had in meeting their rates bills:

> We are finding that very many clients are worse off on income support by £1-3 per week because of the 20 per cent rates which they now have to pay. The national figure of £1.20-1.30 is not enough in Hertmere and I should imagine the same applies in many other higher rateable value areas.[2]

Handicapped (blind) single parent in receipt of invalidity benefit loses free school dinners for 15-year-old son ... loss of income causing great hardship to family. Now also having to pay 20 per cent rates and water rates means that the family is considerably in hardship.[3]

Client is epileptic single man on income support. Been notified by council that he must now pay water rates and 20 per cent general rates, a total of £3.25 per week, and an amenity charge of £6.48. Client's weekly income is £46.97. Client's fuel charges are approximately £11 per week. Client refuses to pay anything towards rates, says he can't afford to.[4]

The obligation to pay 20 per cent rates in combination with other charges in the benefits system has clearly caused considerable hardship. But it is not only a shortage of money, but also administrative problems which have pushed many claimants into arrears.

Since April the backlog of claims in the Housing Benefit Office has caused great distress and problems to many of our claimants. People on income support have *not* been informed about the 20 per cent until mid-summer, causing arrears in the local authority department.[5]

The home-help of Mr A, a man of 89, phoned to say that Mr A could not sleep and had been depressed for a fortnight. Unfortunately Mr A was sent a full demand for his rates instead of a rebated demand and although we telephoned for the rebated demand it has been slow to come. Mr A is quite unable to cope.[6]

Mr H was summonsed for £347 rates arrears. He was married with three children aged between 3 and 8. He suffered from osteo-myelitis and their income consisted of invalidity benefit and child benefit. The arrears had arisen largely due to underpaid housing benefit which we helped Mr H to claim. This reduced his bill to £170... The gist of the Rates Recovery Officer's case seemed to be that, because Mr H had not applied for a rate rebate, as allegedly advised at a previous hearing, he should go to prison. No account was taken of Mr H's difficulty with written English or official forms.[7]

The Convention of Scottish Local Authorities has reported that the majority of local authorities in Scotland are now sending out gross poll tax bills from which any rebate due will be deducted at a later stage. As the case studies above illustrate, unrebated bills can cause tremendous anxiety, as people sometimes wrongly assume they are liable for the whole bill when in fact a rebate is due.[8] Inadequate administration of benefit means people are sometimes taken to court because of arrears for which they are not responsible. Newham Rights Centre reported that some rebates were not paid on time or were incorrectly calculated. They called for the local council not to take court action against people for rent or rates arrears caused by delays in housing benefit payments.[9]

There is a risk that under the poll tax the pressure on local authorities will make these administrative problems worse. The administration of poll tax rebates will be more complicated because of the increased caseload, and because the caseload will consist of a greater proportion of people whose circumstances will change more rapidly (for example, young non-householders and families with children). Moreover, the fact that many people are paying local taxes for the first time adds to the difficulties. As the Convention of Scottish Local Authorities has already reported:

> Despite promotional leaflets, information notes and general publicity on the subject of ... community charge rebates ... it is likely that many of these 'first time payers' will not apply for a rebate until the Summary Warrant has been taken and the Sheriff Officer has started proceedings ... it is also highly unlikely that councils will be in a position to issue monthly reminders.[10]

Arrears

The difficulty of paying the 20 per cent contribution to rates, in combination with the other cuts in housing benefit and rent rises in some authorities, has pushed up the overall level of rent and rate arrears in local authorities. Council tenants pay rates as part of their rent; therefore, any rise in 'rent' arrears may in fact be wholly or partly due to people not paying their rates. A number of reports published recently have shown the scale of the rises in 'rent' arrears since April 1988 in different authorities. The Northern Consortium of Housing Authorities (in the Northern region of England) found that rent arrears rose by 47 per cent between 31 March and 30 November 1988;[11] in metropolitan authorities there was a rise of 37.5 per cent in rent arrears;[12] the *Observer*'s survey of a selection of local authorities showed a rise of 48.5 per cent;[13] while the Welsh District Councils recorded a rise of 48 per cent.[14]

Nor are the problems confined to local authorities. A study of four large housing associations recorded a 20 per cent rise in 'rent' arrears between April and July 1988.[15] The study blames the rise in arrears on the requirement that claimants should pay 20 per cent of their rates and all their water rates. The authors predict that the level of arrears (8-10 per cent of annual rent income) will remain the same at least until the end of 1989:

> The main reason why arrears are rising is not inefficiencies in management or administration, but simply that many households do not have enough money.[16]

We conducted a small-scale survey of local authorities. The results highlighted some of the problems individual local authorities are experiencing. Authorities reported an increase in the proportion of council tenancies in rent arrears and an increase in the amounts of those arrears ('rent arrears' here include rate arrears).

London Borough of Greenwich
* In November 1987, 56 per cent of council tenancies were in arrears.
* In November 1988, 69 per cent of council tenancies were in arrears.
* The level of arrears rose by 67 per cent over the same period. Greenwich attributed this rise to changes in housing benefit.

The London Borough of Wandsworth
* In November 1987, 47 per cent of council tenancies were in arrears.
* In November 1988, 55 per cent of council tenancies were in arrears.
* The level of arrears rose by 19 per cent over the same period. Wandsworth attributed the rise to changes in housing benefit and social security.

Grimsby City Council
* In November 1987, 12 per cent of council tenancies were in arrears.
* In November 1988, 20 per cent of council tenancies were in arrears.
* The level of arrears rose by 58 per cent over the same period.

Harlow City Council
* In November 1987, 48 per cent of council tenancies were in arrears.
* In November 1988, 50 per cent of council tenancies were in arrears.
* The level of arrears rose by 81 per cent.

These examples represent a massive increase in indebtedness resulting in large part from central government social security policies. For local authorities, one of the frustrating aspects of this process is that they themselves are often blamed — even by ministers themselves — for the high level of arrears.

The local authorities' response

Local authorities have a number of powers to allow them to enforce payment of rates and rents. The types of action local authorities in England and Wales may take against people with rate and rent arrears are described below.

Dealing with rate arrears
The local authority may take the following steps if the ratepayer does not pay at each stage:
● Send reminders. If the bill is unpaid after seven days, the local

authority may make a complaint to the magistrates' court.
- The magistrates' court then issues a summons.
- The local authority may then apply for a distress warrant (which is a warning that the local authority will send in bailiffs).
- The local authority then sends in bailiffs who will remove goods by distraint and put them up for sale to meet the outstanding debt, the costs of application and warrant.
- If there are insufficient funds to meet the debt, there has to be a 'means enquiry' to establish the financial circumstances of the debtor. The debt can be remitted in whole or in part.
- If there is 'wilful refusal' or 'culpable neglect', imprisonment may follow.

The major difference to this procedure in Scotland, both previously under rates and now under the poll tax, is that there is no imprisonment for non-payment of the poll tax (see Chapter 10 for a detailed explanation of how the poll tax is recovered in Scotland).

Dealing with rent arrears

In some cases local authorities may recover rates under the same procedure as rent, if liability to pay rates is part of the tenancy agreement. The local authority may take the following steps if the rent-payer does not pay at each stage:

- Send reminders.
- Issue a notice to quit or an intention to seek possession.
- Apply to the county court for a possession order.
- Evict on the basis of a possession order.

The case studies below illustrate some of these powers in action:

Single parent with two young children evicted because of failure to pay council rent arrears, which had increased because of failure to pay 20 per cent rates and water rates.[17]

Client, a single parent, had substantial rent arrears which were being paid by direct deductions from her income support. She had not paid her 20 per cent rates at all since April 1988. St Albans District Council have now threatened her with eviction if she does not pay the arrears of rent, which she is unable to do. If she merely owed *rates* they would not be able to seek repossession, but only distraint or imprisonment. It seems sharp (but legal) to use the rent arrears as a lever to get the rates paid.[18]

Our survey was not extensive enough to see whether local authorities had generally increased or decreased the use of the sanctions available to them in response to mounting arrears, as practice varied from local authority to local authority (with some going out of their way to adopt sympathetic procedures). However, as the examples below show, in some areas there were clear indications of a more extensive use of some sanctions against rate or rent arrears after the April 1988 social security changes.

Local authority action on arrears

Bury City Council
Comparing 1987/88 and 1988/89:[19]
* There was a 28 per cent increase in the number of reminder letters.
* There was a 23 per cent increase in the number of summonses sent out on the first round.
* There was a 12 per cent increase in the number of distress warrants sent out.

London Borough of Lewisham
Comparing 1987/88 and 1988/89:
* There was an increase of 82 per cent in notices of intention to seek possession for rent arrears.
* There was an increase of 217 per cent in evictions, from 24 to 76.

London Borough of Greenwich
Comparing 1987/88 and 1988/89:
* There was an increase of 54 per cent in the number of notices to quit/possession orders.
* There were nine evictions between April and June 1987 and 12 over the same period in 1988.

Grimsby City Council
Comparing 1987/88 and 1988/89:
* There was an increase in the number of intention to seek possession orders of 58 per cent from 327 to 517.
* There was a rise in the number of evictions from 10 to 16.

A survey by the social services department of Hereford and Worcester shows that there has been an increase in the use of bailiffs in the summer of 1988 and reveals the hardship and fear suffered by claimants as a result. A picture of chaos is painted as claimants are thrown from the district council's housing department to social services and on to the bailiffs. The survey looked at 29 cases. The majority were families with children living on income support or family credit, half of whom were single parents. Debts ranged from £20 to £30. Some of the children were on the 'at risk' register, and in four cases the bailiffs distrained goods. Here are two examples from the survey:

One-parent family on income support with three children aged 17, 15 and 7, and eight months' pregnant. Defaulted on £15 per fortnight, while waiting for rent book. Used the money to pay for the gas bill. Notice of distress was sent out from bailiffs for £87.44 rent and rates arrears and costs of £11.91, if this was not settled by 13 August. Client paid £30. Bailiffs came while client was at the hospital. £126.28 outstanding in addition to the cost of the bailiff's van for £46. Client paid £10.93. Client then visited social services department and bailiffs delayed suggesting client gets a loan or help from a relative.

A couple with four children had been on income support but were no longer eligible as the husband was working 24 hours or more a week. They had applied for family credit but not yet received it and were living on his low wages and child benefit. Also there was some confusion over a housing benefit application. The couple had agreed earlier to pay £5 per week to housing department but defaulted after the first payment. Housing department and bailiffs refused to discuss any offer.

The sanctions available to local authorities induce considerable fear. A survey by Stoke on Trent Citizens' Advice Bureau[20] shows how the fear of being imprisoned for rates can be used to intimidate claimants, forcing them to make payments and often pushing them into taking out loans which they cannot afford:

> Many people view the prospect of a court appearance with dread. A summons to the magistrates' court is particularly frightening. The practical and social consequences of the seizure of furniture by bailiffs is particularly draconian and where a threat of this kind is used merely as an administrative convenience by a rating authority, we feel it is entirely unjustified. As increasing numbers of elderly people suffer debt and financial hardship the numbers of pensioners going before the courts for the first time in their lives will increase.

In the period between 1979 and 1987, 3,869 people were actually imprisoned for debt due to rates default in Great Britain.[21] The fear of such treatment hangs over many more. This problem is likely to be even worse under the poll tax, because many of those who are worst off will find a flat-rate tax harder to pay. The Stoke on Trent survey also illustrates that local authorities' powers to write off rates arrears on the grounds of poverty are rarely used:[22]

> It is clear that poverty is not seen by local authorities or magistrates as sufficient grounds for remittance.

This is confirmed by our own survey. With the exception of Islington Council, the local authorities we surveyed generally appeared to use these powers rarely. In any case, when the poll tax is introduced, the power to remit the tax on the grounds of poverty is being abolished.

Conclusion

> The minimum contribution proposed by the Government will be on average a very modest proportion of household income, but it will help to strengthen awareness of local policies and priorities. This is an indispensable part of a healthy local democracy.[23]

Ministers have consistently argued that the 20 per cent contribution is an essential component of local democracy. It can, of course, be argued that a universal financial contribution is a way of encouraging everyone to participate in local authority financial decisions. But in practice the introduction of the 20 per cent contribution to the rates, in conjunction with other social security cuts, has caused severe hardship and anxiety. Local authorities have had to use their powers in an effort to enforce payment, so that many claimants have experienced for the first time the threat or the reality of court proceedings. In truth, the picture of people struggling on minimal incomes to pay 20 per cent of their rates, under threat of legal sanctions, accords poorly with the idea of enabling individuals to make a genuine contribution to the financial decision-making of their local authority. Far from increasing local accountability, this measure seems simply to have increased hardship and insecurity.

The problems of hardship are likely to be worse under the poll tax. The poll tax will fall most harshly on the poor. Local authorities have new and extensive powers, for the first time, to deduct payments for poll tax arrears directly from income support and earnings, thereby further reducing claimants' disposable income. It will be up to the local authority to decide whether it wishes to recover arrears through direct deductions or through distraint of personal goods. It may well be that if claimants fall into serious debt, local authorities will opt for distraint. In addition, the number of people entitled to poll tax rebates will be a much larger and more transient group of people than those currently entitled to housing benefit. As well as possibly causing a lower level of rebate take-up, these features may well result in more mistakes and errors of payment, and a consequent further increase in arrears and in the use of legal sanctions against claimants.

This first taste of a change which has affected the relationship between claimants and local authorities bodes ill for the poll tax.

Notes

1   Douglas Mason, *Revising the Rating System*, Adam Smith Institute, 1985.
2   Citizens' Advice Bureau (CAB) in the Chilterns area.
3   CAB in Prescott area.
4   CAB in south London.
5   CAB in Cardiff area.
6   CAB in Chilterns area.
7   CAB in Stoke on Trent area, quoted in *Jailed for Debt*, Stoke on Trent CAB, 1988.
8   Convention of Scottish Local Authorities, Executive Committee Meeting item, 3 March 1989.
9   *Poor Families Face Bailiffs*, Report by Newham Rights Centre, 1988.
10 See note 8.
11 Unpublished table.
12 *Observer*, 18 December 1988.
13 See note 12.
14 *Housing*, August 1988.
15 *Public Finance and Accountancy*, 24 March 1989.
16 *The Social Security Act and rent arrears in housing associations*, National Federation of Housing Associations Research Report No 2, 1989.
17 CAB in the East Midlands area.
18 CAB in Chilterns area. Note: this procedure is lawful if the payment of rates is part of the tenancy agreement.
19 The information from local authorities related to different dates; however, in each separate case the period of time in 1987/88 was comparable with the following year.
20 *Jailed for Debt, A report on the imprisonment of rates defaulters*, Stoke on Trent CAB, 1988.
21 *House of Commons Hansard*, 22 March 1989, col 646.
22 They have these powers under Section 53 of the General Rates Act 1967, (which can be used to write off debts in exceptional circumstances — such as severe poverty).
23 *The Reform of Social Security*, White Paper, Cmnd 9691, HMSO 1985.

5   Social security on target?

The government has repeatedly argued that a reformed structure of means-tested benefits can target resources more effectively on those most in need. But, in practice, have resources been targeted on the least well-off?

PART ONE
TARGETING

Family credit is the flagship of the government's social security reforms — the supreme example of targeting in practice. Ministers predicted that 60 per cent would take up family credit, in contrast to the 50 per cent who had taken up family income supplement. They estimated that a total of 750,000 families would be *entitled* to family credit; yet the latest government figures show that only 285,000 families were receiving it at the end of 1988/89 — a take-up rate of 38 per cent.[1] Since then, the government has reworked its estimates of the number of families eligible for family credit and now says that take-up is running at about 50 per cent.[2] The benefit has been dogged by delays; the 16-page-long form and the need for detailed information from both claimants and employers has meant an average of 23 working days to process a claim.[3] The government has now simplified the form and launched a major advertising campaign in an attempt to promote take-up.

Some families on family credit, who also claim housing benefit, have suffered considerable overall losses because their family credit is taken into account when calculating housing benefit. The severity of this 'clawback' has been worsened by the cuts in housing benefit under the Social Security Act 1986. Those on rent and rate rebates lose 85 per cent of the value of their family credit in this way. For example, a couple with two children (under 11) with earnings as low as £100 per week, paying average rent and rates, will have *lost* £10.15 per week in real terms as a result of the interaction between family credit and housing benefit.[4]

A further difficulty is that the government's notion of targeting is solely concerned with family (and household) income. Means-tested benefits are assessed on a *family's* income. Yet one important cause of 'hidden' poverty, mainly affecting women and children, is the unequal sharing of resources within households.[5] National insurance benefits, by contrast, are not means-tested but are based on an individual's contribution record. This means that where, for example, a married woman claims unemployment benefit (a national insurance benefit), she can receive this regardless of family income provided she has made sufficient contributions.[6] Thus, the erosion of national insurance benefits over recent years has tended to deprive married women of an income of their own. One example of this is the restriction in eligibility for unemployment benefit and the phasing out of children's additions.

Fortunately, the government did eventually agree to pay family credit to the main carer (usually mothers), rather than to the 'breadwinner' as originally proposed. But the freezing of child benefit for two years running — frequently the only income for a mother not in paid work — has meant many women having less money for their children. As one mother explained:

> My husband is on a small wage. I rely every week on my child benefit to buy food for my three children, my husband and myself. It is not a fringe benefit for us, it is an absolute essential, as I never receive any housekeeping from my husband; all his wages go on the mortgage repayments, gas, electricity bills, etc.[7]

In 1987, 6,545,000 women received child benefit, in comparison with 135,000 men.[8]

Inevitably, the expansion of means-tested benefits brings with it the problem of the 'poverty trap'. The poverty trap is a term used to describe the way in which direct tax on increased earnings combines with the loss of means-tested benefits, to mean that a large proportion of any extra earnings is lost. Although the worst effects of the poverty trap have been eliminated by the new Social Security Act, it has extended a less severe poverty trap to more people.[9] For someone on family credit, 70 pence of every extra net pound earned is lost through reduced benefit — it is only when earnings are high enough to take the claimant beyond entitlement to family credit that the severe poverty trap ends. This disincentive to increase hours of work or earnings clashes with the objective of the new social security reforms to increase self-reliance.

The idea of targeting resources on those most in need through means testing seems to rely on a rather simplistic idea of how benefits work in practice. It takes insufficient account of the needs of individuals within families who may receive unequal shares of resources, and of the practical effects of the interaction between means-tested benefits, and between those benefits and earnings. Above all, it either ignores or makes unjustifiably optimistic assumptions about take-up.

Take-up

In table 5.1, we show estimated take-up rates for some of the main benefits. Three conclusions stand out. Firstly, universal and national insurance benefits perform far better in this respect than means-tested ones: for example, child benefit hits its 'target' almost unfailingly, whereas family credit is missing badly. Secondly, some of the new benefits introduced in April 1988 have performed particularly poorly to date. As we have seen, family credit has a very low take-up rate. In the case of the social fund, we cannot measure take-up in the same way — because there is no *entitlement* to payments which can act as a benchmark. However, it is striking that social fund payments have not even reached the level which the government budgeted for — even though this budget was itself well below the level at which single payments were being paid out under the supplementary benefit scheme. Thus claimants have not even been paid the limited amount theoretically on offer from the social fund. There are some indications that take-up of income support may be below government expectations, but official figures are not yet available.[10] Thirdly, about a quarter of people entitled to housing benefit did not receive it. As poll tax rebates are very similar to housing benefit, this throws open the question of how effectively such rebates can relate the poll tax to ability to pay.

A recent study commissioned by the DHSS identified three principal factors behind the failure of claimants to claim benefits: uncertainty about eligibility, their feelings about the claiming process and finally the claimants' belief that they did not need the benefit (often claimants who were in great need did not claim):

> We believe the roots lie in generally unfavourable attitudes towards the idea of benefit support. In other words there is an underlying feeling about being on means-tested benefits, that eventually inhibits the claim.[11]

As the authors make clear, the causes of low take-up appear to apply almost exclusively to means-tested benefits. In order to make targeting effective, the government's rationalisation of means-tested benefits needed to overcome these obstacles: the evidence so far is that the attempt has not been successful.

The poor take-up of means-tested benefits may be a particularly serious problem for ethnic minorities and for women. There is growing evidence that take-up of benefits among the black and ethnic minority population is lower than for white people.[12] Low take-up may be a

Table 5.1:   Take-up rates of benefits

Date	Benefit	Number receiving benefit	Number not receiving benefit	Take-up rate[*]	Amount underspent/ overspent for relevant year
Means-tested benefits					
Benefits before April 1988 changes					
1983/84[1]	Family income supplement	205,000	175,000	54%	- £55m
1983[1]	Supplementary benefit	4,090,000	1,290,000	76%	- £570m
1984[1]	Housing benefit	6,380,000	1,910,000	77%	- £500m
Benefits after April 1988 changes					
1988/89[2]	Family credit	285,000	465,000	38%	+ £13m
		285,000	285,000	50%	
1988/89[3]	Social fund loans	–	–	87%	- £18m
1988/89[3]	Social fund grants	–	–	33%	- £20m
1988/89[4]	Income support	4,215,000	N/A	N/A	N/A
Non-means-tested benefits					
1987/88[5]	Child benefit	11,799,000	241,000	98%	–
1988/89[6]	Unemployment benefit	620,000	–	close to 100%	–
1988/89[6]	Retirement pension	9,720,000	–	close to 100%	–

[*]   Take-up here implies 'caseload' take-up (the proportion of claimants who take up their entitlement). For the social fund there are no figures for 'caseload' take-up because there is no entitlement as such to loans/grants — we used the proportion of the social fund budget which had been spent.

Sources
1   *The Government's Expenditure Plans 1988/89-1990/91,* Cmnd 288. The take-up estimate of family income supplement is 50% when it is averaged over ten years.
2   There are two estimates of take-up of family credit. The government initially estimated that 750,000 families would be eligible. However, following persistently low take-up figures, it has reworked its estimates of eligibility, saying that the earlier estimates were too high. It now estimates that take-up is running at around 50%: *House of Commons Hansard*, 17 March 1989, cols 391-2; and 23 March, cols 784-5.
3   Most of the money spent on social fund loans will be recouped in future years. *House of Commons Hansard*, 22 March 1989, col 678.
4   There are no estimates available for the take-up of income support.
5   *House of Commons Hansard*, 14 November 1988, col 441.
6   *The Government's Expenditure Plans 1989-90 to 1991-92,* Cmnd 615.

product of a number of factors: fear of the link between DSS offices and the Home Office to check immigration status; racism encountered in DSS offices; language difficulties; ignorance of eligibility; pride in self-reliance, and so on. In a recent study, migrant workers explained their reasons for not claiming benefits:

> ...you go to the DSS, if you are foreign, even if you have the right to claim something, you know you might be asked to fill in one, two, three forms, which you might not understand and fill in wrongly.[13]

There is some evidence to show that claiming means-tested benefits can raise difficult issues within families about the 'breadwinning' role. Again, the DHSS report said that in some couples women do not claim means-tested benefits because they are seen as undermining the husband's role as provider for the family:

> There is evidence to show that some men find it difficult to admit that they cannot provide for their families' needs and hence, in some way, prevent the claim occurring.[14]

This following statement made by one mother graphically illustrates the predicament:

> I rely on [child benefit] totally for the children's upkeep... As it is at the moment, I find it hard to manage with what I'm given. I dread to think what it would be like without it. If benefit had to be claimed similarly to social security, my husband wouldn't allow me to, as he objects to hand-outs — and I'm sure we would be above the poverty line. The way benefit is now, that everyone is entitled to it, is the best policy...[15]

To be successful, benefits need to take full account of the context in which they are to operate. Means-tested benefits in the wake of the April 1988 changes do not appear to take sufficient account of the justified fears of members of ethnic minorities of bureaucracy and racial oppression. Nor have they yet proved capable of meeting the requirements of women for a secure source of income with which they can provide for the needs of their children.

Taxation

The government's argument in favour of targeting benefits through greater use of means-tested benefits tends to focus exclusively on social security expenditure in relation to the distribution of incomes. However, government policy on taxation is of equal importance in determining how income is distributed. Looking at social security in isolation can result in absurd conclusions. For example, the Green Paper on the *Reform of Social Security* concluded that child benefit was not sufficiently well-targeted on poor families, and that greater priority should be given to means-tested forms of family support. Yet the recent review of the tax treatment of couples did not treat targeting as an important objective: under the new arrangements to be implemented in 1990, all married men will continue to receive an additional tax allowance, even if they have no children. The allowance — to be renamed the 'married couple's allowance' — will continue to be of most benefit to the highest earners and of no benefit to those too poor to have taxable income.[16]

Alongside the welfare provided through social security, huge sums are spent on tax subsidies which go mainly to the better-off — often known as 'fiscal welfare'. Mortgage interest tax relief is a glaring example of this inconsistency in the government's concept of targeting. While over £6.75 billion is spent on this relief each year (benefiting the better-off most), housing benefit has been subject to stringent cuts.[17]

In our assessment of the effects of the April 1988 social security changes in the next part of this chapter, we include the changes to direct taxation which were introduced simultaneously (and which were announced in the March 1988 budget — see box). In so doing we take account of the possibility that some of those adversely affected by the social security changes may have experienced a compensatory improvement in their tax position. We also get closer to an assessment of the real effects of government policies on incomes, rather than considering one set of measures in isolation. In our view an approach which seeks to target resources on the least well-off must take into account the distributional consequences of taxes — especially allowances and reliefs — as well as of benefits.

The March 1988 income tax changes

The most important changes in the 1988 budget affected income tax. Personal tax allowances were uprated by twice the rate of inflation. The basic rate of income tax was reduced from 27 pence in the pound to 25 pence. There were also large cuts for higher-rate taxpayers. Indeed, all higher rates were abolished, except for the lowest one — 40 pence in the pound. Previously, the top rate had been 60 pence.

PART TWO
THE IMPACT OF THE APRIL 1988 CHANGES

In the introduction to this book, we quoted a figure referred to frequently by ministers: 88 per cent of people either gained or experienced no change in their cash incomes as a result of the April 1988 changes. Interestingly, the government itself produced figures, less often quoted, which showed that in structural terms (ie, *excluding* the transitional cash protection) only 37 per cent of people gained.[18] Below we provide an alternative analysis of the gains and losses as a result of the social security and tax changes introduced in 1988.

Using a microcomputer model of the tax and social security system (Taxmod 6.7), designed at the London School of Economics, we have examined the effects of a series of social security and tax changes. In the box (page 56) we explain how we modelled the policy changes on the computer.

Table 5.2: Ready Reckoner
How families with different needs are grouped together into decile groups (weekly income after direct taxes and benefits in 1988/89)

	Single person	Couple	Single parent + 1 child	Couple + 2 children
Decile group:				
Bottom	0-£40.55	0-£64.88	0-£56.77	0-£97.32
Second (up to:)	£51.05	£81.68	£71.47	£122.52
Third (up to:)	£60.50	£96.80	£84.70	£145.20
Fourth (up to:)	£73.95	£118.32	£103.53	£177.48
Fifth (up to:)	£89.70	£143.52	£125.58	£215.28
Sixth (up to:)	£106.15	£169.84	£148.61	£254.76
Seventh (up to:)	£126.15	£201.84	£176.61	£302.76
Eighth (up to:)	£154.60	£247.36	£216.44	£371.04
Ninth (up to:)	£197.25	£315.60	£276.15	£473.40
Top	£197.25+	£315.60+	£276.15+	£473.40+

Gains and losses

In order to make a comparison between the tax/benefit system before and after the April 1988 changes, we needed to adjust the 1987/88 benefit and taxation rates. Otherwise the uprating built into the 1988/89 system for inflation would ensure that the reformed system automatically *appeared* more generous than the old. Following John

USING TAXMOD

Taxmod uses data from the 'Family Expenditure Survey', an annual survey of expenditure patterns and living standards in the United Kingdom.[19] The model ignores the social fund and 'transitional protection' which was made available as a *temporary* cushion from cash losses resulting from the April 1988 benefit changes; so it is looking at the *structural* effects of the changes and not at their immediate impact on cash incomes. We do not include the changes to personal taxation which are to be introduced in 1990.

Tax Units

The model assesses income changes in relation to 'tax units' rather than individuals or families. A tax unit is a single person or a couple, along with any dependent children. For simplicity we often refer to tax units in this book as 'families', but it is important to remember that the term includes single people with no dependants. We refer to tax units which include children as 'families with children'. The gains or losses which Taxmod calculates for the sample (some 5,800 families) are projected to give an estimate of the effects of the policy changes under examination on the whole population.

Measurements of Income

We use Taxmod to assess gains and losses for different types of families in terms of their 'equivalent net income'. Net income is the family's income from all sources (including benefits), less direct and local taxes: income tax, national insurance and rates/poll tax are all deducted. Taxmod then allows us to make an adjustment to the income received by those units which include couples or children. This adjustment gives a figure (known as the 'equivalent' figure) which allows a direct comparison between the incomes received by these families and the incomes received by single people. If this adjustment for equivalence were not made, it would appear that a couple with two children and a net income of £100 per week was better off than a single person who had no dependants and a net weekly income of £95 per week — which would clearly be misleading.[20]

Decile Groups

Taxmod divides families ranked according to equivalent net income into ten equal groups, known as 'decile groups'. The bottom decile therefore contains the 10 per cent of families with the lowest equivalent net incomes. The second decile contains the 10 per cent of families who are next poorest; and the top decile contains the 10 per cent of families with the highest equivalent net income and so on. This procedure enables us to see what effect a set of policy changes has on families at different levels on the income scale — from the richest group to the poorest.

The 'ready reckoner' (Table 5.2) shows which decile group different types of families fall into at various levels of income in 1988/89 (after direct taxes and benefits). For example, a couple with a weekly net income of £315.60 or more is in the top decile; a couple with two children with a weekly income of between £122.53 and £145.20 falls into the third decile.

Hills' approach (in *Changing Tax*, CPAG Ltd, 1989), we have uprated benefits, and tax allowances and bands, which applied before April 1988 in line with the most recent estimate of the rise in national income ('money GDP') between 1987/88 and 1988/89. The rise in national income is a measure of economic growth (it assumes no population change). In order for claimants to share in the benefits of economic growth, their benefits would have to keep pace with rising living standards. In recognition of this, until 1980 the long-term national insurance benefits such as retirement pension were uprated in line with the annual increase in earnings or prices, whichever was the higher. We have chosen the rise in national income as the fairest way of measuring how people's incomes have fared in relation to the whole economy.

As far as benefits are concerned, using national income implies that a neutral position would be one in which rates were annually uprated in line with national income, and the rules of entitlement remained the same. Similarly, in relation to direct taxes, our approach assumes that a neutral position would be one in which allowances and tax bands were uprated in line with national income while tax rates and other rules remained the same. The effect of this approach is that a reform is treated as neutral for a particular group of families (such as the bottom decile) if it results in their receiving the same proportion of national income as previously: they are shown as gaining if their share of income goes up, and losing if it goes down. We use the most recent estimate for the rise in national income between 1987/88 and 1988/89, a figure of approximately 11 per cent.[21]

Before and after April 1988

The combined effects of the April 1988 benefit and income tax changes are shown in table 5.3 and figure 5.1. The heaviest losers are in the third decile group — they would be on average £4.01 per week better off under the pre-April 1988 system than they are under the 1988/89 system. This lends support to the fears shared by many Conservative backbench MPs that the biggest losers under a policy of greater targeting would be the 'near poor' — those judged to be sufficiently well off to manage with less help from the state.

But the poorest groups have not benefited instead. Indeed, families in the bottom decile lose on average £1.82 per week, and those in the second decile lose an average of £3.95. This is despite the fact that there is a net cost to the Exchequer of some £1.5 billion in moving from the 1987/88 system to the 1988/89 one. So where has the money gone? The solution to this paradox, of course, lies in the effects of tax cuts on high-income groups. Close to 100 per cent of families in the top decile are better off after the April 1988 changes,

as are 93 per cent of families in the ninth decile. The net average gain
for the top decile is a startling £16.92 per week.

**Figure 5.1 The April 1988 benefit and tax changes: Average gains and losses per
week**

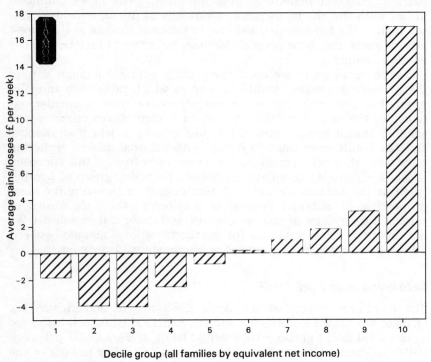

Note: This graph shows the impact of the April 1988 budget and social security
changes.

The strong message of these figures is that the overall consequence of
the social security and tax changes introduced in April 1988 has been
a massive and sudden shift of income from the worse-off to the
better-off.

Table 5.3: The impact of the April 1988 benefit and tax changes

	Losses (£ per week)		Gains (£ per week)		Average gain/loss per week
	£5 +	£5-0	£0-5	£5+	
Bottom decile	11%	48%	24%	2%	- £1.82
Second decile	34%	55%	5%	2%	- £3.95
Third decile	34%	59%	3%	1%	- £4.01
Fourth decile	15%	59%	21%	1%	- £2.52
Fifth decile	4%	47%	45%	1%	- £0.83
Sixth decile	2%	30%	66%	0	£0.16
Seventh decile	1%	23%	75%	1%	£0.97
Eighth decile	1%	15%	78%	5%	£1.78
Ninth decile	0	6%	78%	15%	£3.10
Tenth decile	0	0	34%	66%	£16.92
Overall % gainers/losers	10%	34%	43%	9%	£0.98

Figures do not add up to 100 due to rounding and the exclusion of 'families' where there was no change of income.

Conclusion

It can be said in defence of these measures that the shift in resources from the poor to the rich has only partially occurred in cash terms. Some of the losses for the worst-off took the form of a failure to uprate benefits in line with inflation; some of them take the form of not receiving a share of increased national income; and, where entitlement was cut in cash terms, this was sometimes offset by the temporary payment of a transitional addition. All these points are true, but they do not alter the basic conclusion of our analysis: that the cumulative effect of the tax and benefit measures introduced in April 1988 was to reduce the share of resources going to the poorest groups and increase the share going to the most affluent.

This is also the practical context in which the government's commitment to a policy of targeting through means-tested benefits should be viewed. True, the average losses for the very poorest are slightly less severe in absolute terms than the losses of the 'near poor'. But the policy of targeting appears to have failed even to protect — let alone improve — the incomes of those most in need. Instead, government policy has in practice targeted extra money on those least in need, at the very top of the income scale.

At the outset of this chapter we looked at some of the problems associated with means-tested benefits, in particular low take-up and the poverty trap. These thorny difficulties challenge the notion that such benefits can increase independence and self-reliance. In addition, this failure of means-tested benefits to achieve targeting resources on the poor is compounded by their failure to work efficiently even for those entitled to them.

Notes

1   *House of Commons Hansard*, 23 March 1989, cols 783-4.
2   *House of Commons Hansard*, 17 March 1989, cols 391-2.
3   *House of Commons Hansard*, 6 December 1988, col 124.
4   *House of Commons Hansard*, 4 February 1988, cols 737-42.
5   Julia Brannen and Gail Wilson (eds), *Give and Take in Families — studies in resource distribution*, Allen and Unwin 1987.
6   For more information on entitlement to non-means-tested benefits, see *The Rights Guide to Non-Means-Tested Benefits*, 1989/90, CPAG Ltd.
7   Mrs W, quoted in *Dear Mr Moore* for Save Child Benefit, CPAG Ltd 1989.
8   *House of Commons Hansard*, 9 December 1988, col 384.
9   *House of Commons Hansard*,
10 *Guardian*, 31 October 1988.
11 C Davies and J Ritchie, *Tipping the Balance*, DHSS Report No 16, HMSO 1988.
12 C Brown, *Black and White*, Policy Studies Institute, Gower 1984.
13 N Ardill and N Cross, *Undocumented Lives*, Runnymede Trust 1988.
14 See note 11.
15 Mother of two, Cheshire, quoted in R Lister and A Walsh, *Mother's Lifeline, a survey of how mothers use and value child benefit*, CPAG 1985.
16 *The Reform of Personal Taxation*, Green Paper, Cmnd 9756, March 1986.
17 *House of Commons Hansard*, 15 May 1989, cols 15-16.
18 *Impact of the Reformed Structure of Income Related Benefits*, DHSS, October 1987. The 'structural' impact measures claimants' disposable incomes under the reformed benefit system with what they might have been if the old benefit system had been retained (excluding transitional protection).
19 Taxmod simulates the effects of policy changes by recalculating taxes and benefits for a sample drawn from the 'Family Expenditure Survey 1982'.
20 Adjustment is made to net incomes according to these 'equivalence ratios'. The unit's income is divided by: 1 for a single person; 1.6 for a couple; and 0.4 for each child.
21 *The Government's Expenditure Plans 1989-1990 to 1991-92*, Chapter 21, Supplementary Analyses and Index.

6 The effect of the poll tax on living standards

The fundamental criticism of the poll tax is that it is unfair. The government has sought to demonstrate that this criticism is unfounded. In this chapter we assess the impact of the poll tax on living standards and compare our results with the government's figures.

Factors which affect gainers and losers from the poll tax

Three factors determine whether someone is likely to gain or lose from the introduction of the poll tax: household size, local authority area and the rateable value of property. Firstly, the larger the household's size, the more likely it is to lose under the poll tax — this is because rates are a household tax and the poll tax is an individual tax. At present in England and Wales, a household of four adults will pay one rates bill for the household; in future they will pay four separate poll tax bills. Of course, the converse is also true. Households with only one adult — such as single pensioners or one-parent families — are less likely to lose. Secondly, the poll tax will vary from local authority to local authority. Gains or losses depend on whether the level of the old average rate bill (per adult) is lower or higher than the poll tax charged by the authority. More deprived local authorities, such as those in Inner London, will have higher poll tax bills, in contrast to local authorities in less deprived areas, such as the shire counties. Therefore, people in areas where the poll tax will be particularly high will be more likely to lose from the transition. Thirdly, the lower the rateable value of the property presently occupied, the more likely the person is to lose from the poll tax. People in low-rated properties tend to have lower incomes, so they are more likely to lose from the poll tax.

All three factors interact. For example, an elderly widow living on her own in a home with a high rateable value in the South East is likely to gain from the poll tax. However, a single parent in a low rateable property, living in Inner London, is likely to lose. The low rateable value of the property and the area in which she lives (probably with a high poll tax may outweigh the fact that she is a single adult household.

Modelling the poll tax

A uniform poll tax

We use 'Taxmod', the computer model used previously, to assess the impact of the poll tax. Unfortunately, it is not possible to use Taxmod to model the effects of a *variable* poll tax — that is, one where the precise level of the poll tax varies from one local authority area to another. Our results are therefore based on the assumption that everyone pays an average amount of £234. The actual figure for the national average poll tax is lower than the government's projected figure. Simply to use government projections of poll tax levels could seriously distort the analysis, because of differences between the Taxmod sample and the data on which government figures are based. Taxmod incorporates Northern Ireland, where in fact the rates are continuing. It also seems likely that Taxmod slightly underestimates the average rates per household. We have compensated for this effect by basing our poll tax figure on the Taxmod rates data, rather than directly on government projections.[1]

It would clearly be preferable to use a variable poll tax, since the poll tax is well above average in deprived areas (where families on low incomes are concentrated) and below average in less deprived areas.[2] The use of an average figure therefore tends to underestimate the regressive nature of the poll tax, because it underestimates the burden on poorer families. It also tends to underestimate the scale of gains and losses, because the effect of some people moving from paying very low (or no) rates to very high poll tax bills, or vice versa, is lost. However, in both cases Taxmod's limitations favour the government's case that the poll tax is a fair tax. Therefore, any criticism of the poll tax as regressive can be securely founded on these figures.

Moreover, there are two advantages to using an average figure. Firstly, the projected average poll tax remains the same whether 'safety nets' are included within the analysis or not (see pp 93-94).[3] This means that we do not have the problem of the analysis being distorted by safety nets — or of producing figures which are only applicable after a transitional period of up to five years. Secondly, ministers have laid considerable emphasis on the fact that under the new financial regime local authorities in each area could provide a standard package of services for a uniform level of poll tax. It is debatable whether such a standard package can actually be costed with sufficient accuracy by central government to make this a legitimate claim, because of the difficulty of relating expenditure to local needs, which are so variable.[4] Nevertheless, our analysis shows what the distributional effects would be of a uniform poll tax, and so throws interesting light on this part of the government's argument. Overall, we believe that the use of an average figure allows us to make a fair (if incomplete) evaluation of the effects of the poll tax.

It is also worth bearing in mind that our analysis takes no account of the additional revenue required to fund the increased costs associated with the poll tax. We do not incorporate increases in taxation (whether in the poll tax or central government taxes) to meet the massively increased costs of collection, or to fund the costs of extra rebate payments.

The poll tax on its own

In order to make a direct and uncomplicated comparison between the poll tax and rates, we have first of all modelled the effects of replacing the domestic rates with a uniform poll tax, assuming no other changes to the structure or rates of taxation and social security.[5] Despite the fact that spending on rebates goes up,[6] because the poll tax falls so heavily on the poor, and because there are more payers, nevertheless, 55 per cent of *all* families still lose from the change to the poll tax. One-fifth lose more than £4 a week. Table 6.1 shows the proportion of losers and gainers in each decile group.[7] It is particularly noticeable that over three-quarters of families in the poorest decile are worse off, while over 70 per cent of those in the richest decile gain.

Table 6.1: The impact of the poll tax (without benefit changes)

	Losses (£ per week)		Gains (£ per week)		Average gain/loss £ per week
	£4 +	£0-£4	£0-£4	£4 +	
Bottom decile	11%	68%	14%	7%	- 0.57
Second decile	8%	50%	34%	4%	- 0.15
Third decile	12%	37%	43%	5%	- 0.29
Fourth decile	25%	29%	37%	8%	- 0.74
Fifth decile	34%	33%	23%	9%	- 1.19
Sixth decile	33%	30%	25%	11%	- 0.94
Seventh decile	32%	28%	26%	14%	- 0.63
Eighth decile	23%	28%	30%	19%	0.17
Ninth decile	20%	23%	34%	23%	1.02
Top decile	9%	19%	32%	40%	3.65
Overall % losers/gainers	21%	35%	30%	14%	0.03

Figures do not add up to 100 due to rounding and the exclusion of 'families' where there was no change of income.

Only families in the top three deciles show an average gain from the poll tax (see figure 6.1). The greatest average loss is in the fifth decile (just below the mid-point) at £1.19 per week. But the average loss for the bottom decile is also significant — £0.57 per week.

Figure 6.1 The impact of the poll tax (without any benefit changes) 1988/89: proportions of gainers and losers

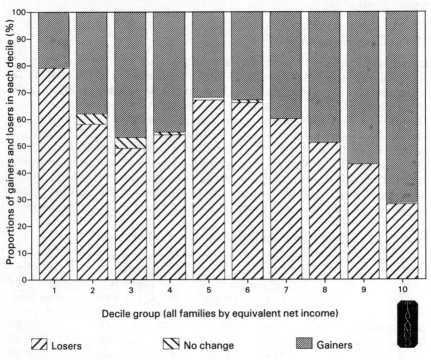

Note: This graph shows the impact of a flat-rate poll tax, with benefits and national taxes unchanged.

The picture which emerges shows how the vast majority of the poorest families lose — but fairly small amounts on average. In the middle of the income range, a slightly smaller proportion (around two-thirds of families) lose, but their losses are larger — approximately one-third of these families lose more than £4 a week. This concentration of larger losses in the middle of the income distribution is probably due to two factors. On the one hand, rebates are not payable at these levels; while, on the other hand, families in this income range pay lower average rates than the better-off groups (because rates do tend to increase with income, albeit slowly). These figures therefore confirm the fears that have been expressed about the effects of the poll tax on the 'near poor' — those who are not well off, but who are not poor enough to qualify for rebates.

The Rt Hon Michael Heseltine MP linked the effect of the poll tax on the 'near poor' to the government's objective of encouraging people away from reliance on state-provided welfare:

> Modern Conservatism has widened its appeal by embracing the instincts of those who want independence and self-reliance. If there is a pivotal point at which the political pendulum is hinged, it is that group of people who have lifted themselves not to great wealth, but clear of dependency on the state and into a position of self-reliance — the council tenants who have bought their homes, the newly self-employed and the thrifty who have saved for their retirement. It is those people, still living in the old terraced houses on council estates everywhere which the local rateable value reflects as being on low incomes, who will suffer disproportionately from the government's proposals.[8]

Nevertheless, we should not lose sight of the fact that the poll tax proves to be more regressive than the rates *throughout* the income scale — each of the seven decile groups which lose are worse off than the three richest groups which gain from replacing the rates with a poll tax. This is despite the fact that we are evaluating a uniform poll tax, which is less regressive than a variable one. This finding contradicts the claim in the government's Green Paper that, in relation to ability to pay, the poll tax 'would perform no worse than the rates'.[9]

Poll tax rebates: protection for the poor?

Evaluated on its own merits, the poll tax is more regressive than the rates. The government has argued that poll tax rebates offer protection for the poor from the flat-rate poll tax. But this argument is also open to several objections.

We have seen how the take-up rate for means-tested benefits, including housing benefit, is very poor (see Chapter 5). The likelihood is that take-up of poll tax rebates will be even worse, particularly at the beginning, when the new tax is unfamiliar. The poll tax will bring many more people into eligibility for rebates by extending the net of taxation and raising the tax bills of the poor. In fact, the government estimates that over 11 million individuals will be entitled to poll tax rebates (see Chapter 1, table 1.1). Many of these people will have no experience of claiming rebates: ignorance, confusion or pride may prevent them from taking up their entitlement.

One indication of the problems that lie in store is that Scottish authorities have already reported disappointingly low take-up figures. For example, in Strathclyde (covering almost half of all Scottish poll tax payers) the council had calculated that around 580,000 adults would be entitled to rebates. But by the time the tax was introduced only around 60 per cent of these had applied.[10] The Convention of Scottish Local Authorities (COSLA) estimated that throughout Scotland only 478,000 rebate applications were made before the start of the new tax, out of the 1.1 million people entitled. In some areas, take-up was said to be as low as 25 per cent.[11] Some late applications for rebates may be backdated to 1 April 1989, but certainly the rebates scheme has got off to a very bad start.[12]

Rebate take-up is significantly worse for private tenants (only 53 per cent take up their entitlement to housing benefit), probably because their landlords are unaware of, or unconcerned about, their benefit entitlements.[13] Their poll tax payments will be separated from their rent payments. This is likely to reduce still further the proportion of taxpayers with landlords who check their eligibility for rebates. The poll tax falls heavily on non-householders. Evidence from the Institute for Fiscal Studies showed that take-up of supplementary benefit was considerably lower for non-householders than householders. It is likely that this pattern may be repeated for poll tax rebates.[14]

It is not only non-householders who are less likely to take up their benefits, but also people in employment, according to a study by the DSS.[15] People in work entitled to a small amount of poll tax rebate — the very people whose needs the government aimed to meet through its concession on rebates — are less likely to claim their benefit. If they do not claim they will be left to pay their poll tax bills in full. Another group, who have to meet the poll tax without the help of rebates at all, are those people from abroad who are admitted to Britain subject to the requirement that they do not have recourse to public funds. Poll tax rebates count as public funds. As we show later in this chapter, black people and ethnic minorities are more likely to face higher poll tax bills and to have least money with which to pay them. A minority within this population will be denied access to rebates altogether — leaving them to meet the poll tax in full.

A further objection is that rebates can only imperfectly relate a flat-rate tax to ability to pay. They leave those who have low incomes, but who are not poor enough to qualify for rebates, paying the same as those on the highest incomes. The government has tried to meet this criticism by producing figures to support its view that, taking into account the improvement to the rebate scheme, the poll tax performs no worse than the rates as far as ability to pay is concerned. We turn now to consider the validity of these figures.

The problems with the government's figures

The government has produced figures comparing the poll tax and the rates which take benefit changes into account.[16] They do so in the way that most supports their case for the poll tax.

The figures show that as a result of the introduction of the poll tax, 52 per cent of *tax units* gain and 49 per cent lose; while 58 per cent of *households* gain and 42 per cent lose. They show that the poll tax is on average a smaller proportion of equivalent net household income than domestic rates for each income group except one: households with net incomes between £100 and £150 per week.[17]

There are a number of problems with these figures. Firstly, the comparison is based on the amount of net rates payable after the April 1988 housing benefit cuts, which included the introduction of 20 per cent rates payments; and estimates net poll tax payments taking into account the improvement to the rebate taper to be introduced with the poll tax (see Chapter 2). Ministers have refused to compare the position before the 20 per cent minimum rate contribution was introduced, with the position under the poll tax.[18]

Secondly, the figures for *households* show the poll tax in the most favourable light. The reason for the difference between the figures based on tax units and households is that tax units (consisting of a single person or a couple, along with any children) are often smaller than households. There may be several tax units within a household. However, since the poll tax falls on individuals rather than households, a single person or even a couple may be worse off even though they live in a household which gains overall; figures which relate to households disguise this effect. A household analysis effectively assumes that resources are shared within the household. Moreover, in a household analysis three or four adults who live together count as one loser (almost all such households lose from the poll tax), whereas three or four adults who live separately from each other count as three or four gainers (the majority of single people living alone gain). Analysis by tax unit does not entirely resolve this problem, since it gives the same weight to a couple as to a single person; but it is preferable to analysis by household because it is usually a smaller unit and therefore closer to the actual impact of the poll tax.[19]

Thirdly, the figures are also based on the assumption that everyone takes up their entitlement to rebates whereas, in fact, take-up of rebates is quite poor (see Chapter 5). This assumption underestimates the number of losers, by exaggerating the gains from the reduction in the rebate taper from 20 per cent to 15 per cent and from the extension of rebates to non-householders. Some of those who 'gain' in the government figures because of rebates are in fact people who do not claim rebates at all.

A fourth point is that the government's figures adjust 1989/90 benefit rates to 1988/89 prices, deflating means-tested benefits by 4.7 per cent, and other benefits by 5.9 per cent.[20] This presumes that uprating benefits in line with prices preserves a 'neutral position', even though it usually means that benefits decline in value relative to national income. Moreover, the actual inflation figures used seriously understate projections of price increases between 1988/89 and 1989/90. By April 1989 inflation was already running at 8 per cent. This means that the government's poll tax figures disguise a fall in the real value of benefits.

Finally, the government figures assume that the change from domestic rates to the poll tax does not result in an increase in average local tax bills. This assumption is at variance with other government figures for England (see note 1) and has already proved to be inaccurate in Scotland, where poll tax bills are significantly higher in real terms than the last rate bills.

The poll tax with benefit changes

We have conducted a similar exercise to the government's, attempting to eliminate some of the flaws identified above. Our figures compare the actual position in 1988/89 (with the rates, and claimants paying 20 per cent contributions) with what would have happened had the poll tax been introduced in that year along with the associated benefit changes. The figures relate to tax units rather than households and are again based on a uniform poll tax of £234 (see box for other assumptions).

Assumptions

We have adjusted 1989/90 benefit rates to 1988/89 prices; we have deflated all benefits by 7.5 per cent. This was the rate of price inflation in January 1989 (when the analysis was carried out).[21] In conducting this exercise, we have assumed that benefit take-up remains constant with the switch from rates to poll tax.

The results of this analysis are strikingly different from those published by the government. Sixty-three per cent of families lose and only 37 per cent are better off. Moreover, losers are heavily concentrated among the poorest groups: 83 per cent of the bottom decile lose, with an average loss of £1.04 per week; 79 per cent of the second decile are also worse off, and in this decile the average loss is £1.02 per week. By contrast, 71 per cent of families in the top decile are better off, and here the average change is a gain of £3.65 per week (see table 6.2 and figure 6.2).

The pattern of average losses and gains that we saw when considering the poll tax without any changes to the benefits system is repeated. The greatest average loss in absolute terms is the £1.72 per week experienced by families in the fifth decile. However, the losses for the poorest families actually make up a greater proportion of their income.

Table 6.2: The impact of the poll tax (with associated benefit changes)

	Losses (£ per week)		Gains (£ per week)		Average gain/loss £ per week
	£5+	£0-£5	0-£5	£5+	
Bottom decile	2%	81%	12%	4%	– 1.04
Second decile	4%	75%	18%	2%	– 1.02
Third decile	5%	69%	23%	1%	– 0.98
Fourth decile	9%	63%	22%	4%	– 1.44
Fifth decile	9%	62%	22%	5%	– 1.72
Sixth decile	8%	60%	25%	6%	– 1.39
Seventh decile	6%	57%	28%	9%	– 0.95
Eighth decile	5%	48%	35%	12%	– 0.08
Ninth decile	4%	41%	38%	17%	0.87
Top decile	2%	27%	36%	35%	3.65
Overall % losers/gainers	9%	54%	27%	9%	– 0.41

Figures have been rounded and 'families' excluded where no change of income.

Families with children (see table 6.3 and figure 6.3)

The impact on families with children (including one-parent families) is particularly worrying. Remembering that our use of a uniform poll tax tends to underestimate the scale of the gains and losses, it is quite remarkable that the poorest third of all families with children with incomes of £75 or less a week lose more than £1.50 on average in the same period. Meanwhile, 2.9 per cent of families with children with equivalent net incomes of over £250 per week gain on average £6.77 per week. Overall, 63 per cent of families with children are worse off.

Figures published by the government confirm this conclusion regarding families with children. The government's figures show that poorer couples with children are more likely to be losers than gainers. Fifty-six per cent of couples with children lose from the poll tax (although poorer single parents gain overall from the poll tax according to the same figures).[22] Women are likely to bear the burden of trying to make ends meet in the context of these losses, and we now turn to a consideration of the specific impact of the poll tax on women.

Figure 6.2 The impact of the poll tax 1988/89: with associated benefit changes (average gains and losses per week)

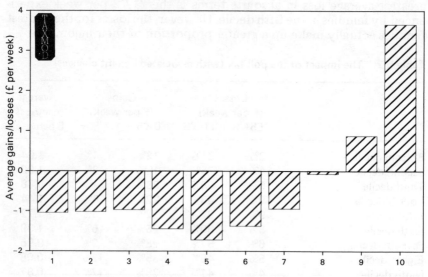

Decile group (all families by equivalent net income)

Note: This graph shows the impact of a flat-rate poll tax and includes the impact of the April 1989 benefit uprating (deflated to 1988/89 prices), and of the 15 per cent poll tax rebate taper.

Table 6.3: The impact of the poll tax on families with children (with associated benefit changes)

Income range (£ per week)	Proportion in each income range%	Average gain/loss (£ per week)
up to £50.00	14	– 1.52
£75.00	22	– 1.54
£100.00	23	– 1.12
£125.00	16	– 0.69
£150.00	10	0.58
£175.00	6	1.36
£200.00	3	1.91
£225.00	2	3.35
£250.00	1	4.05
£250.00+	3	6.77

Note that these groupings are not deciles, and the lower income ranges contain more families.

Figure 6.3 The impact of the poll tax on families with children (with associated benefit changes) 1988/89: Average gains and losses per week by income group

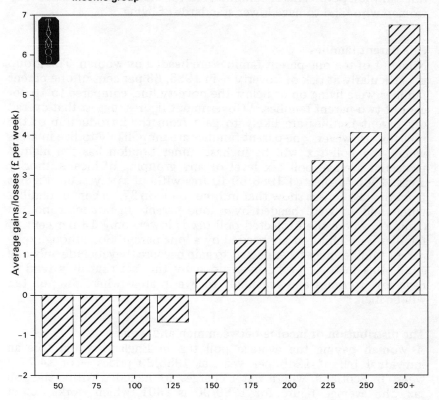

Top equivalent net income for each group of families with children

Note: This graph shows the impact of a flat-rate poll tax and includes the impact of the April 1989 benefit uprating (deflated to 1988/89 prices) and of the 15 per cent poll tax rebate taper.

The impact of the poll tax on women

Women are more at risk of poverty than men. They earn on average two-thirds of men's weekly wages; they are more likely to be on income support; their unemployment has risen faster than men's; and the cost of unpaid caring which women have traditionally taken on is inadequately recognised by the welfare state. As our analysis has shown, because the poll tax is flat rate, it takes a larger share of the income of the poor than the rich. Women who pay their own poll tax bill will be particularly badly hit because of the greater likelihood that they are poor. This is compounded for black and ethnic minority women who tend to have lower standards of living.

One-parent families
Nine out of ten one-parent families are headed by women. This group is particularly at risk of poverty — in 1985, 63 per cent of one-parent families were living on or below the poverty line, compared to 10 per cent of two-parent families.[23] Government figures suggest that overall one-parent families are likely to gain from the introduction of the poll tax. However, one-parent families are more likely to live in areas where the poll tax will be highest. Inner London has the highest projected average poll tax level of any grouping of local authority areas: £506 (projected 1988/89 figures without safety nets). Figures from the last census show that in Inner London 27 per cent of families with children were headed by a lone parent. In non-metropolitan counties, where the projected poll tax is lower, only 13 per cent of families with children are headed by a lone parent. So, although one-parent families may be expected to gain because they include only one adult, this factor may be overridden by the fact that they tend to have low incomes and are likely to live in areas where the poll tax will be high.[24]

The distribution of income between men and women
A woman paying the average poll tax in England would face an individual bill of £246 per year, at 1988/89 prices — or £4.77 a week. In Scotland, where water charges are included within the poll tax, the average figure for 1989/90 is £301, which works out at £5.79 per week.[25]

Women in couples without their own incomes will have to ask their husbands or male partners to pay these bills for them. As we have seen, although the poll tax is levied on individuals, married or cohabiting women have no entitlement to rebates if their partners have a high enough income to pay the poll tax (see Chapter 2). According to government estimates, 2.9 million women over the age of 18 have no regular income of their own from employment, investment or state benefits (excluding child benefit).[26] In 1986, 60 per cent of married women with a child under 5 were not doing paid work.[27] These women will have either to persuade their partners to pay the poll tax for them, or use the very small incomes they may have from sources other than earnings — mainly child benefit. Thus the proclaimed objective of 'independent' taxation under the poll tax is not matched by the likely reality. Although couples are independently taxed, in practice the woman may often be dependent on the man to pay her bill.

The government's own figures show that female-headed households are concentrated in the income range where net poll tax payments are higher than rates — 34 per cent of female-headed households (or 1,170,000 women) fall into this category.[28]

The poll tax may have significant implications for how money is divided within couples. Some research has been done to show which member of a couple pays the rates bill at the moment. Jan Pahl's study on family finances shows that women are more likely to pay rates in households with low incomes, while men are more likely to pay in households with high incomes (see table 6.4). In low-income households (with income below £134 per week), 56 per cent of the wives took responsibility for paying rates bills, but only 30 per cent of the husbands did so. In medium-income households (with incomes of £135-£211 per week), there was a more even spread — in 34 per cent of households wives paid, while in 36 per cent husbands were responsible. In high-income households the pattern was reversed: in 68 per cent of households husbands paid and 21 per cent of wives paid.[29]

Table 6.4: **Responsibility for paying rates by total household income (percentages)**

Rates paid by	Income (£ per week)		
	Low under £134	Medium £135-211	High £212 and over
Wife	56	34	21
Husband	30	36	68
Either/both	15	30	11
Total number in sample	27	44	19

The government has, in part, based its case for the poll tax on the assumptions that rates are paid by heads of households, and that other family members are unaware of the level of local taxation. Other figures produced by Jan Pahl throw interesting light on this argument. She has devised a general framework within which the division of money between husbands and wives can be analysed. Within this framework, there are four main patterns of money management. Firstly, there is 'wife management', where the woman handles all the money. This pattern tends to prevail in poorer households. Secondly, there is the 'allowance' system, where wives are given a housekeeping allowance from their husbands. Thirdly, in a 'shared management' arrangement both share responsibility for income and expenditure. Finally, 'independent management' implies that the husband and wife keep separate income and expenditure. Table 6.5 shows that the wife is more likely to pay rates where she manages the finances and the husband is more likely to pay rates in an allowance system.

Table 6.5: Responsibility for paying rates by system of money management (numbers)

Rates paid by	Wife management	Allowance system	Shared management	Independent management
Wife	11	7	15	1
Husband	0	13	18	6
Either/both	1	1	16	1
Total number	12	21	49	8

Jan Pahl shows that in a majority of two-adult households rates are either paid by women who are not the main breadwinners, or are paid in the context of two partners sharing responsibility for finances. Nevertheless, the government may be right to believe that the poll tax may change the way that local tax bills are met by couples and, if so, it appears likely that women will end up paying a greater share than they have done under the rates.

If, on the other hand, patterns of money management remain largely unaltered, then we would expect that in the majority of low-income households the husband would hand his poll tax bill over to the wife to pay. In high-income households the pattern would be reversed. As Jan Pahl comments:

> Thus in households where it will be hardest to find the money to pay the poll tax, it will be women who will be faced with finding that money.[30]

The impact of the poll tax on black and ethnic minorities

Just as women are at greater risk of poverty and therefore will be hard hit by the poll tax, so too are black people and ethnic minorities. Beset by much higher rates of unemployment, lower wages and greater dependence upon benefits, black people and ethnic minorities will frequently have to meet the poll tax from below average incomes.

They are also more likely to be living in areas where the poll tax will be highest. Government projections of poll tax levels in England (in 1988/89) put the poll tax at an average of £258 in the metropolitan districts compared with £222 in the shire counties, and £326 in Greater London.[31] The majority of black people and ethnic minorities live in London or other metropolitan areas: 80 per cent of Afro-Caribbeans live in a London borough or metropolitan district, as do 75 per cent of Bangladeshis, 71 per cent of Pakistanis, and 68 per cent of Africans. These figures compare with 31 per cent of whites living in these metropolitan areas.[32] So the majority of black people and ethnic minorities will face higher than average poll tax bills, and have less money with which to meet them. The position is made much worse by the concentration of people from black and ethnic minorities in Inner London, where the average poll tax is projected to be £506 (1988/89 prices). As noted above, the projected average poll tax for the whole of Greater London is £326 per year — 35 per cent above the average for England as a whole. More than two-fifths of people who are black or from an ethnic minority live in Greater London (and indeed the majority of these live in Inner London). By contrast, around one-tenth (11 per cent) of white people live in Greater London.

A study by the Association of London Authorities analysed gainers and losers in London by race.[33] The authors found that over two-thirds of all ethnic minority households would lose from the poll tax compared with just over half of all households. These findings are summarised in figure 6.4.

Family characteristics
The concentration of black and ethnic minority households in areas where the projected poll tax levels are higher than average is compounded by the fact that a disproportionate number of these households also include three or more adults. Government figures illustrate how people who live in larger households are more likely to be losers from the poll tax. According to their figures, 75 per cent of households with three or more adults (1,825,000 households) lose from the poll tax, compared with 25 per cent who gain.[34] A survey conducted by the Policy Studies Institute found that 17 per cent of Afro-Caribbeans and 22 per cent of Asian people lived in households with more than three adults; this is compared with 6 per cent of white people.[35]

The black and ethnic minority population is also a younger population. Young people living at home with their families lose heavily by the poll tax, because they are having to pay a local tax for the first time. This effect will be intensified for young Afro-Caribbeans who have especially high rates of unemployment.[36] Twenty-eight per

Figure 6.4 The poll tax in London: proportion of gainers and loses in each ethnic group (by household)

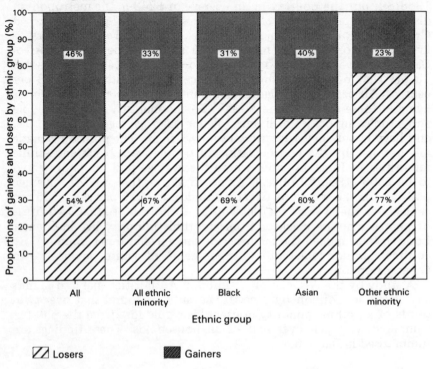

Ethnic group

 Losers   Gainers

Source: Association of London Authorities, Black people, Ethnic minorities and the poll tax, 1988.

cent of the ethnic minority population is aged between 16 and 29 years compared with 20 per cent of the white population.[37] High unemployment and the poll tax are likely to reinforce the feeling and experience that some young black people already have of exclusion from society — especially as they follow fast on the heels of the social security changes which have been particularly directed at young people (see Chapter 2).

Conclusion

The government claims that the poll tax is no more regressive than the rates, and that rebates will provide adequate protection for the poor. We have found that this is not borne out by statistical comparisons, and that further doubt is cast upon the fairness of the poll tax by consideration of the way housing benefit has worked in the past — particularly the low level of take-up of rebates.

We have compared the poll tax with the rates in isolation from any benefit changes and found that, although such a change involves extra public expenditure on rebates, only the rich gain; the poor lose significantly, and the middle-income groups lose most. Next, we have examined the possibility that these losses for the worst-off would be offset by changes to the benefit system, and found that the improvement to the rebate scheme did not protect the position of the poor. In considering the position of women, the research findings that we considered show that in poorer couples it is most likely to be the woman who is responsible for paying rate bills. We believe that the poll tax may add to the burden these women bear of attempting to manage inadequate family budgets. Finally, other evidence shows that black and ethnic minority households are likely to be worse affected by the poll tax than their white counterparts, because they are more likely to live in metropolitan areas (particularly in Inner London) and more often include more than two adults.

In summary, the poll tax *is* more regressive than the rates, and involves a cut in living standards for poor and middle-income families. This is the case even when changes to the system of benefits are taken into account. It has a particularly severe impact on low-income families with children, and is likely to bear heavily on two vulnerable sections of the community — women and ethnic minorities.

Notes

1 Government projections assume that the average poll tax in England in 1988/89 would have been somewhat higher than the average rate bill per adult (£246 rather than £239). The difference arises because English authorities used balances (ie, money held over from previous years) to keep rates down in 1988/89. Government projections take account of the need to fund part of this shortfall by levying higher poll taxes. However, the part which would need to be funded by the business rate is not accounted for in government figures, which means that in order to fund current expenditure either government grant, or the business rate, or the poll tax would have to be higher than the government's calculations indicate. In Scotland, the actual poll taxes levied in 1989/90 have turned out to be substantially higher than the average rates for the previous year, taking inflation into account (see Chapter 9). In order to derive our average figure, we therefore first of all calculated the level of poll tax which would, according to Taxmod, yield the same revenue as the rates — a figure of around £228 per year. We then raised that figure in line with the projected increase in the average tax bill in England, to reach a figure of £234. The assumed increase in local tax bills is significantly below the one which has actually occurred in Scotland with the introduction of the poll tax.

2 The fact that the poll tax is projected to be higher in deprived areas of England and Wales, and has proved to be higher in deprived areas of Scotland, is demonstrated in Chapter 9.

3   See Chapter 8 for an explanation of safety nets. In fact, in the first year of the poll tax, when safety nets have the greatest impact, local authority poll tax levels tend to approximate more closely to the national average.

4   See Chapter 8 for a discussion of the role of central government 'needs assessments' in the new financial system.

5   Entitlement to rebates changes: the fact that the poll tax falls more heavily on the poor, and that there are more payers, causes spending on rebates to go up. Indeed, the increase (of some £340 million) more than offsets the assumed additional revenue from the poll tax, meaning that the change from the rates to the poll tax has a net cost of around £50 million. In turn, this means that the model projects a small average gain to families from the change.

6   Our use of the term 'families' to refer to tax units is the same as in Chapter 5, see p 56.

7   We explain what deciles are in Chapter 5. As in that chapter, our deciles here are based on equivalent net income. Chapter 5 includes a 'ready reckoner' showing how families of different compositions are allocated to particular deciles according to their net incomes (see p 55).

8   *House of Commons Hansard*, 18 April 1988, col 619.

9   *Paying for Local Government*, Green Paper, Cmnd 9714, HMSO, January 1986, para 3.37.

10 *Independent*, 1 April 1989.

11 *Guardian*, 31 March 1989.

12 The government made a temporary concession, allowing councils to backdate (without loss of subsidy) rebate claims received less than eight weeks after the introduction of the poll tax.

13 Housing benefit take-up, technical note, DHSS Statistics and Research Division, 1987.

14 V Fry and G Stark, 'The take-up of supplementary benefit — the gaps in the safety net', *Fiscal Studies*, Vol 8, No 4, November 1987.

15 C Davies & J Ritchie, *Tipping the Balance*, DHSS Report No 16, HMSO 1988.

16 Department of the Environment press release, 15 December 1988.

17 *House of Commons Hansard*, 12 January 1989, cols 743-4. The government has emphasised an analysis based on ranking households by unadjusted net income, which means that the ranking takes no account of household size. This was the only form of analysis included in the Department of the Environment summary figures on gainers and losers published in December 1988. A ranking of households by unadjusted net income has the absurd result of treating a household with four adults, several children and an income of £100 per week as having a higher standard of living than a single person with an income of £95 per week (see Chapter 5). This approach is again helpful to the government's case: since larger households are those most likely to lose under the poll tax, an analysis which presents them as better off makes the tax appear fairer. The one income range in which households on average lose (those with incomes between £100 and £150 per week) also happens to be in the range in which the largest number of households fall (29 per cent of all households, *House of Commons Hansard*, 2 February 1988, col 359). However, in this group, as in all those in the lower half of the income distribution, the average change in household bills is shown in the government figures as small. The government has refused to publish figures showing gainers and losers by decile group.

18 *House of Commons Hansard*, 14 February 1989, cols 193-4.

19 The presumption of the poll tax is that individuals are responsible for their own finances, and in this sense the best solution would be to evaluate the impact of the tax on individuals rather than either households or families.

Unfortunately, neither our analysis nor the government's is capable of producing results at the individual level, and so we are compelled to rely on figures relating to tax units — the next best thing. Individuals losing will be greater than the number of tax units losing.

20 4.7 per cent and 5.9 per cent were the inflation rates between September 1987 and 1988, used to uprate actual benefits to their 1989/90 level.

21 The rate of inflation was in fact very close to the rise in national income, which was predicted to be 7.9 per cent between 1988/89 and 1989/90 by the Chancellor in the Autumn Statement. National income here refers to money GDP. Autumn Statement 1988, HM Treasury, November 1988.

22 *House of Commons Hansard*, 2 February 1988, cols 363-4.

23 *Low Income Families Statistics*, DHSS 1985. In the absence of an official definition of poverty, CPAG has used the supplementary benefit level as a proxy for a poverty line (see C Oppenheim, *Poverty the Facts*, CPAG Ltd 1988).

24 *One-parent families in Great Britain*, Information Sheet, National Council for One Parent Families 1985. The average for Inner London Boroughs excludes the City of London.

25 See Chapter 9.

26 *House of Commons Hansard*, 13 July 1987, col 384.

27 *General Household Survey 1986*, HMSO 1989.

28 *House of Commons Hansard*, 3 March 1989, col 359.

29 In each case in the remaining households no one partner was responsible for paying the bill.

30 J Pahl, *Money and Marriage*, Macmillan, forthcoming 1989.

31 P Esam, *Poll Tax Guide*, LGIU 1989.

32 *Black people, ethnic minorities and the poll tax*, Association of London Authorities 1988.

33 See note 32.

34 Department of the Environment press release, 15 February 1988, Table 10.

35 C Brown, *Black and White*, Policy Studies Institute, Gower 1984.

36 *Employment Gazette*, Department of Employment, December 1988.

37 Refers to the period 1984-86. *Social Trends 1988*, HMSO 1988.

7 The combined effect – the social security changes and the poll tax

The primary concern for a family struggling on an inadequate budget is not whether benefit changes or a new local tax are more or less fair in isolation: what matters for them is the overall effect of government policies. Will they have more or less income to manage with? For this reason we believe that the government should itself evaluate the cumulative impact of its tax and benefit policies on living standards, and here we carry out an exercise of that sort using Taxmod.

The poll tax and the April 1988 changes

To evaluate the interaction of the poll tax with recent social security and tax changes, we compare the net income families would receive under the pre-1988 social security and tax systems with the net income they can expect to receive with a poll tax in force instead of the rates.

Using Taxmod
In order to model the pre-1988 tax/benefit system, we uprate tax allowances and benefit rates in line with the increase in national income between 1987/88 and 1988/89 (see Chapter 5, p 57). And in order to model the poll tax, we assume that a uniform poll tax of £234 is introduced throughout the United Kingdom,[1] taking into account the benefit changes associated with the poll tax by deflating 1989/90 benefit rates to 1988/89 prices (see Chapter 6, pp 62-63); we also introduce the 15 per cent taper for poll tax rebates.[2]

This comparison offers us the opportunity to assess what the cumulative impact of the poll tax is in conjunction with the recent tax and benefit changes. Table 7.1 and figure 7.1 show the average changes in net income for the ten deciles.[3] As in previous analyses, losses are concentrated at the bottom end of the income scale and gains at the top. Indeed, the losses among the poorer families are not due to reductions in the overall level of public spending: in aggregate the changes have a net cost to the Exchequer of some £950 million, largely due to the tax changes. This extra money is 'targeted' on the 30 per cent of families with the highest incomes and, in addition, substantial sums are redistributed to them from the poorest families. Overall the reforms are highly regressive.

Figure 7.1 The impact of poll tax, benefit and tax changes (1987/88-1988/89): average gains and losses per week

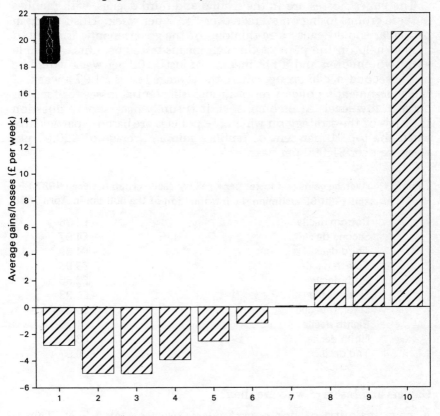

Note: This graph shows the impact of the April 1988 budget and social security changes, in combination with a flat-rate poll tax and the associated benefit changes (ie, the 15 per cent poll tax rebate taper, and the April 1989 social security rates deflated to 1988/89 prices).

Losses and gains are much larger than those resulting either from the April 1988 changes or from the poll tax considered independently (see pp 55-57 for a definition of a 'loss' or 'gain'). Whereas the bottom decile was shown to lose an average of £1.04 per week from the introduction of the poll tax (with the associated benefit changes — see Chapter 6), here the poorest 10 per cent of families lose an average of £2.86 per week. The combined effects of the social security, tax and poll tax changes result in losses for 62 per cent of all families and gains for 38 per cent. One-fifth (20 per cent) lose £5 or more and 8 per cent gain £10 or more.

The largest losses are in the second and third deciles, with families in these groups losing on average over £4.95 per week. This finding in particular should cause a re-thinking of the government's strategy to 'target' help on the poorest through means-tested benefits. A couple with two children and a net income of just £100 per week would be in the second decile group, where the average loss is £4.97 a week. If the government's policies result in such substantial losses for families on such low levels of income, then it is surely necessary to question the basis of the strategy on which the policies are based — particularly when the top 10 per cent of families gain an average of £20.57 per week, or over £1,000 per year.

Table 7.1: Average gains and losses per week by decile group between 1987/88 and 1988/89 assuming the introduction of the poll tax in April 1988

Bottom decile	– £2.86
Second decile	– £4.97
Third decile	– £4.99
Fourth decile	– £3.96
Fifth decile	– £2.55
Sixth decile	– £1.23
Seventh decile	£0.02
Eighth decile	£1.70
Ninth decile	£3.97
Top decile	£20.57

Gainers and losers — who are they?

A huge majority of *non-householders* lose (see table 7.2). This is particularly the case for young people aged between 18 and 25 who will have suffered first from a lower rate of income support and then from the introduction of the poll tax. Older non-householders (aged 25 and above) also have to pay local taxation for the first time. Among householders, *tenants* tend to lose (70 per cent of them are worse off as a result of the changes), whereas owner-occupiers are less likely to do badly (42 per cent lose from the changes): this reflects the lower income of tenants, but also specifically the cuts in rent rebates (housing benefit) which have fallen harshly on tenants.

Table 7.2 gives a summary of the characteristics of gainers and losers. It shows clearly how regressive the changes are. The largest losses are concentrated in families where the head of household's income from earnings and investments is lowest, and the largest gains are in families where income on this measure is highest.

Table 7.2: **Characteristics of gainers and losers: tax and benefit changes between 1987/88 and 1988/89 (with the poll tax)**

	Average weekly income* of head of family	Non-householder	Householder	Tenant	Owner-occupier
Absolute losses					
£6+	£21.75	11%	16%	25%	10%
£4-6	£46.76	26%	12%	16%	9%
£2-4	£96.69	36%	13%	16%	11%
£0-2	£110.34	21%	12%	12%	12%
All losers	£70.10	94%	53%	70%	42%
Absolute gains					
£0-2	£147.42	5%	11%	10%	12%
£2-4	£187.02	1%	9%	7%	11%
£4-6	£203.58	0	8%	6%	9%
£6+	£340.07	under 1%	18%	8%	25%
All gainers	£237.69	6%	47%	30%	58%

*Note: The measure of income used here is different from that used elsewhere in the book. Taxmod here calculates income as the average weekly figure without benefits — ie, primarily earnings and investment income. Percentage figures do not add up due to rounding and because 0.5% of householders, tenants and owner-occupiers experience no change in their income.

'Perverse targeting'

The government has consistently argued that an improvement in the assistance provided to low-income families with children would be one of the main advantages to flow from the new emphasis on targeting. Ministers have thereby sought to justify the shift of expenditure away from child benefit to means-tested forms of support. John Moore MP made the following comment in a speech to the Commons:

I have never made any secret of my belief that [child benefit] is not the most effective use of social security resources... If we were to uprate it across the board, most of the money would go to better-off families, including the very wealthiest. The poorest ... would gain nothing at all from the child benefit increase... That would be *perverse targeting* in the extreme. I have decided therefore as last year to direct help where it is most needed to the lower income families with children. I propose to put substantial additional resources into the benefits going to those families... I firmly believe that it is better to target resources in this way than to improve child benefit for all, including those on the highest incomes.[4] *(our emphasis)*

Our figures show that changes to taxes and benefits do indeed target additional resources on families with children — some £1.1 billion in all — but not on poor families with children. Despite this extra spending, families with children whose equivalent net incomes are below £100 per week actually lose on average: this low-income group accounts for more than half of the total of families with children — 59 per cent in fact (see figure 7.2 and table 7.3). Moreover, the third of families with children on incomes of less than £75 per week (35 per cent) lose on average between £4.88 and £5.01 per week each.[5]

Table 7.3:   The impact of 1988 benefit and tax changes and the poll tax
on families with children (1987/88-1988/89)

	Losses (£ per week)		Gains (£ per week)		Average gain/loss £ per week
	£10 +	£0-£10	0-£10	£10 +	
0–£50.00	18%	67%	14%	2%	- 4.88
– £75.00	13%	73%	13%	1%	- 5.01
– £100.00	2%	61%	34%	2%	- 1.37
– £125.00	1%	40%	56%	1%	0.79
– £150.00	0	22%	68%	9%	3.64
– £175.00	0	11%	72%	17%	5.42
– £200.00	0	8%	60%	32%	7.68
– £225.00	0	0	56%	44%	11.58
– £250.00	0	0	33%	62%	14.62
£250.00 +	0	0	19%	82%	137.59
Overall % losers/gainers	6%	49%	37%	8%	2.99

Figures do not add up to 100 due to rounding and the exclusion of families with children where there was no change of income.

Note: In this table the income ranges do not divide the population into equal groupings.

Figure 7.2 The impact of poll tax, benefit and tax changes on families with children (1987/88 to 1988/89). Proportions of gainers and losers in each income group.

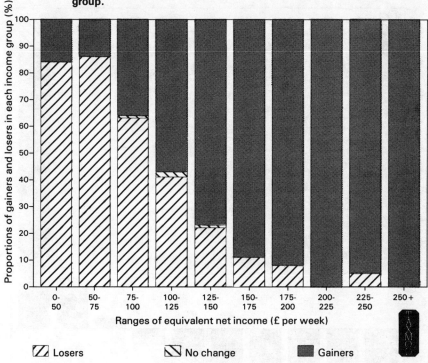

Ranges of equivalent net income (£ per week)

☑ Losers   ◨ No change   ▨ Gainers

Note: This graph shows the impact of the April 1988 budget and social security changes in combination with a flat-rate poll tax and the associated benefit changes (ie, the 15 per cent poll tax rebate taper, and the April 1989 social security rates deflated to 1988/89 prices).

How is it possible for policies to result in a net cost to the government of over £1 billion and yet also to result in such substantial losses for those on lowest incomes? By now the answer is all too familiar. High-income families with children have gained both as a result of the reduction in net revenue received by the government, and through money being redistributed from poorer families to the better-off. Families with net weekly incomes of between £225 and £250 gain an average of £14.62 a week. Over 85 per cent of those with incomes below £75 per week lose, while there are no losers among those with incomes above £200 per week. This is 'perverse targeting' indeed.

Figure 7.3 The impact of benefits, taxes and the poll tax (1978/79–1988/89): average gains and losses per week

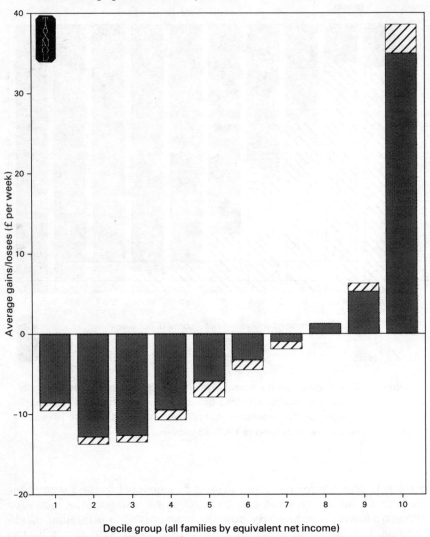

Decile group (all families by equivalent net income)

■ Changes 1978/79–1988/89　　▨ Poll tax

Note: This graph shows the impact of social security and national tax changes between 1978/79 and 1988/89; and the additional impact of a flat-rate poll tax with associated benefit changes (ie, the 15 per cent poll tax rebate taper, and the April 1989 social security rates deflated to 1988/89 prices).

The whole picture

How have social security and tax changes affected families since 1978/79? In his book *Changing Tax*, John Hills compared the 1988/89 tax and benefit system with the one which would have applied had 1978/79 rates of benefit and tax allowances been increased in line with the increase in national income over the ten-year period.[6] He showed that on the basis of this comparison there had been a massive shift of resources from families on low incomes to the better-off. Here we have carried out a similar analysis, but we have added on the effects of the poll tax.[7] The results should not be viewed as an estimate of actual cash gains and losses of families over the period; instead the analysis shows how changes to the tax and benefit system since 1978/79 have affected different groups relative to the growth in the economy as a whole.[8]

Table 7.4:   Gains/losses (£ per week) per household by decile groups between 1978/79 and 1988/89

	1978/79 – 1988/89	1988/89 + poll tax	Total 1978/89 – 1988/89 + poll tax
	(1)	(2)	(3)
Bottom decile	– £8.59	– £1.04	– £9.63
Second decile	– £12.86	– £1.02	– £13.88
Third decile	– £12.08	– £0.98	– £13.06
Fourth decile	– £9.53	– £1.44	– £10.97
Fifth decile	– £5.97	– £1.72	– £7.96
Sixth decile	– £3.19	– £1.39	– £4.58
Seventh decile	– £1.00	– £0.95	– £1.95
Eighth decile	£1.46	– £0.08	£1.38
Ninth decile	£5.31	£0.87	£6.18
Top decile	£34.89	£3.65	£38.54
Revenue gain to government	£1,800m	£640m	£2,440m

Note: In columns 2 and 3 the poll tax is modelled taking account of associated changes to the benefit system, such as the introduction of a 15 per cent rebate taper. See Chapter 6 for a full explanation.

Table 7.4 summarises the results in two stages. It can be seen that for nine of the ten decile groups the poll tax compounds the distributional effects of the previous changes. The 20 per cent of families with the highest incomes gain substantially from the tax and benefit changes made between 1978/79 and 1988/89, and they gain again from the poll tax. Meanwhile, families in the lower seven deciles all lose from the income tax and social security changes — and the poll tax increases their losses. Only in the case of the eighth decile do the effects of the two sets of changes run in opposite directions: the average gain of £1.46 incurred by this group from the benefit and income tax changes is offset to a very minor degree by a loss of £0.08 from the poll tax. This is represented graphically in figure 7.3.

Conclusion

The evidence we have presented paints a bleak picture of the step-by-step changes which have combined to reinforce the division between the poorer and richer sections of society. The distributional effects of the poll tax work to reinforce the regressive nature of changes introduced in April 1988 and during the previous decade. Among those who lose most are low-income families with children, and young people living at home with their parents. Our findings reinforce the importance of drawing together the effects of tax and benefit changes. If reforms are evaluated in isolation the gravity of the reduction in living standards faced by those at the bottom of the income scale is not appreciated. For instance, losses from the introduction of the poll tax alone may appear to be small. But the groups who lose from the social security changes lose once again under the poll tax. Society is becoming increasingly polarised. The combined effect of the social security and tax changes — both at local and national level — is creating an even greater divide between rich and poor.

Notes

1 In fact, as noted in Chapter 6, Taxmod covers the whole of the United Kingdom, so approximately 2 per cent of the sample are families who in fact will not pay the poll tax because they live in Northern Ireland.
2 As in Chapter 6, 1989/90 benefit rates are deflated by approximately 7.5 per cent, see p 68.
3 See Chapter 5 for an explanation of how families are allocated to decile groups on the basis of equivalent net income. As in previous chapters, the term 'families' is used here to refer to all tax units — including single people and couples without children.
4 Rt Hon J Moore MP, *House of Commons Hansard*, 27 October 1988, cols 456-7.
5 These income figures again refer to equivalent net income — see Chapter 5 for an explanation.
6 We use the same basic approach as John Hills' (*Changing Tax*, CPAG Ltd 1988): his exercise was based on Taxmod, used similar assumptions to our own and covered the period between 1978/79 and 1988/89.
7 The comparison between 1978/79 and 1988/89 looks at the difference between taxes and benefits in the current system (1988/89) and those that would have resulted had the 1978/79 system been uprated in line with national income growth (a rise of 172 per cent in money GDP according to the latest

estimates in the *Government's Expenditure Plans 1989-90 to 1991-92*, Cmnd 621, HMSO, January 1989). Generally governments have not committed themselves to uprating benefits by national income growth. However, long-term national insurance benefits such as retirement pension were uprated by earnings or prices, whichever was higher, until 1980: this had a similar effect.

Our figures for the difference between the 1978/79 and 1988/89 tax and benefit structures differ in magnitude from those given by John Hills in *Changing Tax* (section 3), although not in overall distributional effect. The main reason for the discrepancy is that his estimates used the 1988 Budget forecast of national income for 1988/89, whereas we have used the 1988 Autumn Statement estimate, which has been revised upwards. Our 1978/79 benefit levels are thus 272 per cent of their cash levels (whereas he was up-rating by 264 per cent). This means that rather than being revenue neutral as he estimated, the revised estimates incorporate an even faster relative fall in benefits and hence an overall gain to the government of £1.8 billion. A further reason for the difference is that we have used a later edition of TAXMOD which allows for more of the widening in income inequality since 1979 than that used by John Hills. However, some of the higher income at the top of the distribution reflects the abolition of the highest tax rates: it is no longer necessary to convert 'income' into capital gains to avoid tax rates above 40 per cent. As a very approximate way of adjusting for such effects, our '1978/79' tax system incorporates a top income tax rate of 75 per cent, rather than the actual 83 per cent.

8. Families were allocated to decile groups according to their level of income in 1988/89.

8 The new financial system and the regions

The poll tax is being introduced alongside significant changes to local government finance. It is these changes which affect what the level of the poll tax is in different parts of Britain. This chapter explains the technical changes to local government finance and goes on to examine how these changes affect deprived and non-deprived areas.

The government's purported objective for the poll tax is to increase local choice and accountability. We need to look at two questions in order to assess whether the poll tax can meet this objective in deprived areas. Firstly, what impact will the new financial system have on the revenue which local authorities in deprived areas are obliged to raise from local taxpayers, to fund their current level of service provision? Secondly, how will the poll tax affect local authorities' capacity to act against deprivation? Will people living in the more deprived regions of the country be able to afford to vote for the services they need?

The latest changes to local authority finance are taking place in the context of a sharp reduction in central government financial support to local authorities over the last decade. The total amount of grant paid annually by central government to local authorities — known as Aggregate Exchequer Grant — has fallen by £916 million between 1978/79 and 1988/89 (to English authorities).[1] This squeeze has been applied with similar ferocity across the regions: deprived regions have not been singled out for special treatment.

PART ONE
EXPLAINING THE NEW FINANCIAL SYSTEM

The uniform business rate

The first change of major significance is the replacement of the *local* business rate (in England and Wales) by a *national* business rate.

Under the old system, the rate poundage is set individually for each area by local authorities (see box for an explanation of the old

---

Note to box: Scotland — The old system in Scotland was based on similar principles, but the technical arrangements were different.

THE OLD FINANCIAL SYSTEM[2] (ENGLÁND AND WALES)

Calculating rates

Rates are a tax on property. The level at which the rate is set is called the 'rateable poundage' — which is expressed as a number of pence in the pound. Each property has a 'rateable value', which is assessed on the basis of the rent which could be charged for the property if it were let on the open market. Generally, if a property is larger and of better quality, its rateable value will be higher too. The higher the rateable value, the higher the rates bill will be as well. The amount of rates paid on a particular property is calculated by multiplying the rateable value by the rateable poundage. If a property has a rateable value of £200 in an area where the rate poundage is 150 pence, then the rates bill is £300 per year.

Central government grant

The old system of Rate Support Grant is supposed to take account of three main factors: *needs* (the requirement to spend more or less depending on local conditions), *resources* (the capacity of the area to finance services through local taxation) and *local spending*.

Grant-related expenditure assessment (GREA)

The government's needs assessment is known as Grant-Related Expenditure Assessment (GREA). GREA is an assessment made by central government of the variation of needs between different local authority areas, which is used in the distribution of grant. A high GREA in a particular area implies that there is an above-average need for local authority services in that area (for example, due to a large number of elderly people in the population). This should result in an above-average payment of central government grant to that area. The GREA is expressed as the amount of expenditure considered necessary by central government to provide a standard level of services, given the local social and demographic conditions. It has come increasingly to be used prescriptively by central government, with those authorities which spend more than the level of their GREA being described as 'overspenders'.

'Resources equalisation'

The amount of grant each area receives is also adjusted to take account of resources: this is known as 'resources equalisation'. Poorer areas would have to levy the same rate poundage as rich ones if they chose to spend at the level prescribed in government needs assessments (ie, at the level of their GREA). However, properties in these areas tend to have below-average rateable values. Since rate bills are calculated by multiplying rate poundages and rateable values, the rate bills would be lower than in richer areas for equivalent levels of spending. This, in effect, means that there is a subsidy from areas with greater resources (more properties with higher values) to those with lower resources — hence the name 'resources equalisation'.

Spending

Grant also varies to take account of the amount each local authority actually *spends*. The original intention of these variations was that central government should make some contribution to extra local spending, but more recently the system has been used to penalise local authorities which increase their spending.

financial system). Under the new system, the government will set a uniform rate poundage for the whole of England and Wales, which will be roughly equivalent to the average of the old individual poundages.[3] The revenue from this national rate will be pooled by central government and will fund a grant paid to each local authority — the size of which will be proportionate to the number of people living in the area.

In Scotland, the national business rate has not yet been introduced, although there are plans to integrate Scotland into the English and Welsh system. In the short term, other measures have been introduced to achieve similar effects.[4]

The change to a uniform business rate has a number of important effects. Firstly, it alters the revenue available to local authorities and consequently the amount domestic taxpayers must pay in order to sustain the current level of services. Authorities which have in the past had a high level of income from the business rate tend to lose: these are authorities with a concentration of non-domestic properties (such as in the centre of many cities); or those which have non-domestic properties with above-average rateable values; or those which charge an above-average rate poundage (again this is the case in many metropolitan areas).

The second effect is on the 'tax base' which local authorities can rely upon to fund changes in expenditure. Under the old system, local authorities can vary their revenue by raising or reducing taxation on both businesses and residents. Under the new system, however, businesses neither contribute to a local improvement of services nor benefit from a reduction of local taxation. The effects of a change in revenue fall wholly on domestic residents.[5]

Thirdly, the change to the uniform business rate means that in all probability local authority finances will be progressively 'squeezed', forcing local authorities to face a choice between either increasing the poll tax or cutting net expenditure on services. The new system places the decision as to the overall level of business rate payments in the hands of central government. The poundage in England and Wales (and the individual poundages in Scotland) are to increase at best by inflation, and already the government is under pressure from businesses to reduce their level of local taxation. In addition, Malcolm Rifkind, Secretary of State for Scotland, has said that the loss of revenue resulting from the integration of the Scottish business rate with the English and Welsh system will not be fully made up by central government grant. Instead, a 'small proportion' of the lost revenue will have to be 'absorbed' by local authorities: in other words, covered either by cuts in local authority expenditure or increases in revenue.[6] This is an illustration of the way in which central government control of the business rate can be used to squeeze local authority finances.

Moreover, even if the rate poundages were to keep pace with inflation, this would be unlikely to be sufficient to fund a constant share of local authority costs. A very large proportion of local authority costs consist of wages. Even where — as with teachers and police, for example — wage levels are set by central government, these costs tend to rise faster than inflation. Under the new arrangements, the gap between wage costs and inflation cannot be passed on to business ratepayers. Unless central government comes up with additional grant money (see below), poll tax payers, increased charges or service cuts will have to fund the difference.

The new grant system

The second important change to the financial system affecting local government is the abolition of the old grant arrangements (see box).

The *new* grant system is based solely on the government needs assessment, and takes no account of the differences in resources between authority areas.[7] It is intended to ensure that any local authority which spends exactly at the level determined by central government has to levy the *same* level of poll tax. According to Department of the Environment figures, this level would have been £202 in England in 1988/89.[8] This means that, even if they follow central government spending prescriptions, the poorest areas are expected to pay just as high a poll tax as the richest. Inevitably the abolition of 'resources equalisation' is damaging to areas with lower levels of economic activity and wealth, and they tend to lose substantial amounts of grant.

The government is also reviewing the way in which needs are assessed (in England and Wales) with a view to simplifying the system. This review could be used to offset some of the effects of introducing the new grant system — by increasing the needs assessments of those authorities which lose under the new structure. However, the government is not committed to altering the balance of needs in this way.

The new grant arrangements are to be phased in over a period of four years (three to five years in Scotland). During that period, a system of 'safety nets' will operate. In the first year these are intended to ensure that the revenue received in each area from the business rate and from grants remains the same as it would have been under the old system. Temporary assistance for those authorities which will lose when the system is fully operational is to be funded by reductions in grant for those authorities which gain. Over the transitional period safety nets will be gradually phased out.

Safety nets will heavily disguise the impact of the poll tax during its first year. The implication for most authorities is that, if they keep their expenditure approximately the same, they can levy a poll tax close to the average domestic rate (per adult) they were levying in the last year of rates.[9] Of course, this still entails substantial losses for particular individuals and families — for example, for non-householders who have not previously had to pay the rates. Nevertheless, safety nets temporarily soften the blow for families in areas where full implementation entails substantial increases in average local tax bills.

Safety nets are also very important because of the impact they have while they are being phased out. Authorities which eventually face poll taxes higher than their previous average rate level will have to *increase* the poll tax each year for four years, just to maintain their revenue at a constant level. Each year they will face a choice between cutting net expenditure on services or increasing the poll tax — or both. Conversely, authorities which eventually face poll taxes lower than their previous average rate level will be able either to cut the poll tax each year for four years, while maintaining spending on services, or to hold the poll tax steady and spend more, or both. In Scotland, the same points apply over the three- to five-year transitional period there. Over the transitional periods, the causal relationship between spending decisions and poll tax levels, which is supposed to be the basis of accountability, will simply not operate in most areas. The poll tax will reflect changes in the amount of grant received by each authority, rather than spending decisions.

Spending by individual authorities

When we consider individual authorities, a third change in the system of finance is important — new 'precepting' arrangements. Under the old system in England and Wales, upper-tier authorities, such as counties, police and fire authorities, and the Inner London Education Authority (ILEA), do not levy their own rates. Instead, they have money collected for them in the form of a 'precept' by lower-tier authorities (districts and boroughs), who do levy their own rates. The 'precept' is expressed in the form of a rate poundage, and is simply added on to the poundage used to calculate household and business rates bills.

This means that income is derived from districts and boroughs in proportion to the rateable values of the properties within their boundaries. The effect of this is to achieve a form of 'resources equalisation' (see p 91) at local level — with wealthier areas contributing more to 'county'-wide spending than poorer areas. The principles are similar in Scotland, although in practice the arrangements are different, because the upper-tier authorities (the regions) are responsible for rates collection, not the districts.[10]

Under the new system, precepts will be issued in terms of 'pounds per head' of adult population. As a result, poorer areas will have to take over responsibility for expenditure previously funded by their richer neighbours. There is a further complication. In London, the ILEA is to be abolished, which means broadly that responsibility for expenditure will be shared in proportion to educational needs — for example, the number of school-age children.

It is also important to note that the government has retained its powers to cap the revenue raised by particular authorities. Indeed, in England and Wales it has strengthened these powers, instituting a system whereby authorities are capped after they have agreed their annual budgets, rather than being given prior notice of the limit to be applied to them.

Gearing

Under the new system local authorities will have no control over the revenue they receive from business ratepayers, and grant will not vary with expenditure. This gives rise to the major problem that increases in spending at the local level have an exaggerated impact on poll tax bills.

The new system is intended to ensure that any local authority which spends exactly at the level determined by central government has to levy the same level of poll tax. This the system achieves. But, although the poll tax only accounts for a small proportion of local revenue (on average around a quarter), all spending in excess of the government's needs assessment has to be funded by poll tax payers. The result is that a small amount of spending above the level of the government's needs assessment generally results in a large poll tax increase. On average a 5 per cent increase in expenditure requires a 20 per cent increase in the poll tax. This is a fundamental problem because it undermines the government's declared objective of establishing a clearly visible relationship between local spending and local taxation.

Small variations in central government needs assessments have a similarly dramatic effect. Thus, for example, a 10 per cent reduction in the level of a local authority's needs assessment would be likely to cause an increase in the local poll tax of between 25 per cent and 30 per cent. Again this goes to the heart of the question of local account-ability. In theory, the poll tax is supposed to reflect the wishes of local voters, but in practice it is just as dependent on national decisions about grant and local needs.

This problem is often referred to as one of 'gearing' — because it relates to the ratio of changes in spending or grant to changes in taxation.

PART TWO
REGIONAL DEPRIVATION

We now turn to look at the practical impact of these changes at the regional and national level. We have ranked the regions (and nations) of the United Kingdom according to four general indicators of deprivation (see table 8.1). These indicators are: the proportion of households which had gross incomes below £125 per week in 1985-1986,[11] the level of unemployment, the proportion of personal incomes derived from social security benefits, and the regional Gross Domestic Product (GDP) per head as a percentage of the UK GDP per head.

Table 8.1: English regions, Scotland, Wales and N Ireland:
indicators of deprivation

Region/nation	% with gross weekly income under £125[1]	Unemployment[2] %	% of income derived from social security[3]	GDP per head[4] %
N Ireland	44 A	20.8 A	19.4 A	77.4 B
North	42 A	14.7 A	17.0 A	88.9 B
Yorks & Humberside	40 A	11.3 A	16.5 A	92.7 B
Scotland	39 A	13.7 A	14.4 A	94.5 B
North West	38 A	12.9 A	16.1 A	92.8 B
Wales	38 A	12.8 A	17.5 A	82.4 B
West Midlands	38 A	10.0 A	14.8 A	91.6 B
East Midlands	34 –	8.6 B	13.5 A	95.1 B
South West	32 B	7.4 B	12.1 B	94.0 B
East Anglia	31 B	5.4 B	12.3 B	99.8 B
South East	27 B	6.0 B	9.5 B	118.5 A
UK	34	9.6	13.1	100.0

A = above average
B = below average
Sources: 1 Family Expenditure Survey 1986. Based on incomes in 1985 and 1986.
2 Unemployment rate in November 1988 according to the Unemployment Unit measure. Unemployment Unit Briefing, January 1989.
3 As for column 1
4 GDP per head in 1987 as percentage of UK average. *Economic Trends,* November 1988.

This is by no means intended as a definitive deprivation ranking of regions and nations. Nevertheless, the data is sufficient to indicate those regions which face the severest economic and social problems. If we ignore Northern Ireland (which is not affected by the poll tax), then six regions/nations show up negatively on all four indicators: the North, Yorkshire and Humberside, Scotland, the North-West,

Wales and the West Midlands. The East Midlands is the closest to representing an average based on these indicators.[12] In general, the last three regions — the South West, East Anglia and the South East — appear likely to experience the least problems of deprivation.[13]

It needs to be emphasised that by looking at the regional level we gloss over the huge variations which averages conceal. Poverty is a problem throughout the country and, just as in every locality there are some families on low incomes, so in every region there are some deprived neighbourhoods.

The South East illustrates this particular problem. The indicators imply that the South East suffers a level of deprivation considerably below the national average. Yet the 12 Inner London boroughs (excluding the City of London) are among the most deprived areas in the country. It is plain that in order to make sense of the regional impact of the poll tax we need to separate Inner London from the rest of the South East — to treat it as a large area of intense deprivation within a more affluent region.

Average poll tax levels in the regions

There are significant regional differences in the average amounts people have to pay in poll taxes (see table 8.2). The two most deprived English regions will, on the basis of government estimates, have average poll taxes above £260 per person. They are closely followed by the North West, whose average is £250. The comparable figure for Scotland, based on actual 1989/90 poll tax levels, is £261.[14] The others all have averages below £240 — except for Inner London, which has the staggering average of £506 (at 1988/89 prices without safety nets).

So poll tax levels will be higher on average in the deprived regions and Scotland. But is this because rates are already higher in those areas, or because individuals in those areas are on average being made worse off as a result of the introduction of the poll tax? The second column of the table shows that it is losses in net revenue from grant and business rate income in the deprived regions that are causing high poll taxes (see table 8.3). Indeed, Yorkshire and Humberside goes from having the lowest average rate per adult of all the English regions to having the third highest poll tax (after the North and Inner London), an average loss of £62 per adult. The situation in London is particularly striking. Currently, the average rate per adult in Inner London is just £41 higher than that for outer London: according to government projections, the poll tax will widen this gap to £276 per adult.

Table 8.2:   English regions, Scotland and Wales: poll tax levels and
average changes in bills (1988/89 prices)

Regions/nations	Poll tax level[1] £	Average rate per adult[2] £	Average change per adult £
North *	273	215	58
Yorkshire & Humberside *	264	202	62
Scotland *	261	246	15
North West *	250	238	12
Wales *	151	151	0
West Midlands *	219	235	- 16
East Midlands	235	226	9
South West	212	211	1
East Anglia	196	208	- 12
South East[3]	215	262	- 47
— Inner London	506	305	201
— Outer London	230	264	- 34
England	246	239	7

* Above average deprivation

Notes

1   These levels are based on the funding required to fund the current level of services
(1988/89), with full implementation of the new grant system (no safety nets) and the
introduction of the national business rate in England and Wales. They are all government
projections except the Scottish figure. This is based on the actual poll taxes being levied
from April 1989. We have eliminated the effect of safety nets and have deflated the
actual figure net of water charges by 7.5% (the rise in prices during the 12 months to
January 1989). This gives a Scottish figure based on the actual poll taxes levied, but at
1988/89 prices.

2   Figures for average rates per adult derived from: parliamentary answer by John Selwyn
Gummer MP to John Battle MP, 22 December 1988; and parliamentary answer by Ian
Grist MP to Paul Murphy MP, 29 July 1988.

3   Excludes Greater London.

A new financial regime for the regions

These huge changes in average local tax bills occur alongside the
introduction of the poll tax, because of the alterations to the local
government finance system. These changes do not directly affect the
position of Wales and Scotland relative to the English regions. In each
case the changes to the financial systems within those countries are
intended initially to be 'revenue neutral' — neither increasing nor
decreasing the total income of local authorities.

Two aspects of the financial changes are particularly important to the English regions. Firstly, there is the abolition of the local business rate. This change is disastrous for Inner London councils, resulting in a loss of income of over £1,000 million, and largely explaining the exceptionally high poll taxes which are projected in those boroughs. This money is spread — somewhat unevenly — among the English regions (outside Greater London), which all gain something as a result (see table 8.3, column 1).

Table 8.3: English regions: changes in business rate and grant income as a result of the new system of finance (1988/89 prices)

Region	Change in business rate income (£m)	Change in grant income (£m)	Net gain or loss (£m)
North *	50.865	- 206.801	- 155.936
Yorkshire & Humberside *	91.970	- 347.688	- 255.718
North West *	109.386	- 200.624	- 91.238
West Midlands *	133.720	53.598	187.318
East Midlands	75.562	- 119.881	- 44.319
South West	243.495	- 230.280	13.215
East Anglia	81.059	- 40.790	40.269
South East[1]	217.767	307.732	525.139
— Inner London	- 1,017.049	631.898	- 439.151
— Outer London	67.227	153.197	220.424

* Above average deprivation

Note: 1 Excludes Greater London.

Source: Parliamentary answers by Virginia Bottomley MP to David Blunkett MP, 25 November 1988.

However, in the most deprived English regions these gains are more than wiped out by the effects of the new grant system. The damaging effect of the abolition of resources equalisation on regions with lower levels of economic activity can be seen from table 8.3 (column 2). This shows the three most deprived English regions (the North, Yorkshire and Humberside, and the North West) losing £750 million in annual government grant. This is only offset by a relatively small increase in their business rate income (£250 million). In Inner London, grants are projected to increase — but not by enough to compensate for the huge loss of income from the business rate. The position is graphically illustrated in figure 8.1.

Thus the authorities in the more deprived areas of England face a very substantial net loss of revenue from the new financial system. Just as the poll tax threatens to increase economic divisions at the

Figure 8.1   Changes to local government finance: Impact on the English regions

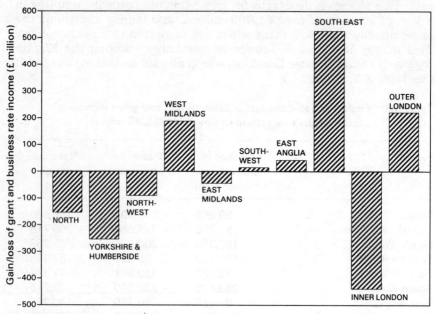

Sources: See notes to table 8.3
Note: Changes in the annual business rate and central government grant income
            of the English regions which would have occurred had the poll tax and the
            new system of finance been introduced in 1988/89

individual level, the new financial system is likely to widen inequalities between the regions. Unless the government decides to use adjustments to the needs assessments to alter the effects of the new system radically, the poorest regions will be losing very substantial amounts of revenue under the new arrangements — and their losses will finance gains for authorities in the more affluent regions.

Moreover, these losses will be phased in over a four-year period, during which time, if authorities in the deprived regions wish to sustain net spending on service provision, they will have to escalate poll tax levels in large annual steps. Many authorities may feel compelled to raise the poll tax each year, but also to attempt to soften the impact of those increases by cutting services. The squeeze in the deprived regions promises to be fierce indeed.

Conclusion

The changes to the financial system which accompany the poll tax are of major importance. The local business rate is being abolished, and a new grant system is to be introduced; the changes are to be phased in over a transitional period.

The new financial system for local government involves a huge transfer of resources out of the poorer regions to finance gains for the less deprived regions. The result is much higher average poll tax bills in the deprived regions than in the better-off regions. In turn, this means poorer families will on average face higher bills than better-off families — because low-income families are concentrated in the deprived regions. Again this shows that the estimates of losses (see Chapters 6 and 7), based on a flat-rate poll tax, were very cautious.

Accountability — defined by the government as creating a visible relationship between poll tax levels and spending — is likely to be blurred by this process of bleeding resources from authorities within the deprived regions. Over the period during which safety nets are phased out, deprived authorities must raise poll tax levels very substantially just to keep services at a standstill. Cuts in services would generally mean not that they could cut poll taxes, but rather that the increases they would have to impose would be slightly smaller. On the other hand, authorities in the more affluent regions will be able to cut poll taxes year by year while spending more on services.

Similarly, accountability is fundamentally undermined by the effects of 'gearing', whereby changes in spending or grant have a disproportionate effect on the poll tax which the authority has to charge. The new system is designed to work if authorities 'choose' to spend at the level prescribed for them by central government needs assessments. But this gives enormous weight to decisions about local needs taken at national level. If local voters want a small improvement in service provision above the level prescribed by central government, they must pay a disproportionate price for it.

Notes

1   *Public Finance and Accountancy*, 4 December 1987. The annual amounts of the Annual Exchequer Grant are revalued in line with prices, taking no account of the greater increase in earnings over the period.

2   Ian Douglas and Steve Lord, *Local government finance: a practical guide*, LGIU 1986.

3   This change will be accompanied by the implementation of a revaluation of

business property (the uniform poundage will in fact be deflated, so that the total revenue from the business rate after the introduction of the new system is roughly the same in real terms as at present). Thus both the rate poundage and the rateable value of business properties will alter, bringing about extreme changes in the bills payable in many cases. However, the government proposes to phase in the gains and losses over a number of years.

4   The amount by which Scottish local authorities can increase their business rate has been capped by the government, and the revenue raised was taken fully into account in the calculation of central government grant to be paid to local authorities for 1989/90. The government is now taking powers to cap the individual business rate poundages levied by particular Scottish authorities, and these powers will be used over an unspecified period of years, to bring Scottish poundages into line with the uniform poundage in England and Wales.

5   This effect applies equally to Scotland as to England and Wales. In Scotland local authorities may not vary the business rate above the maximum level set for them by the Secretary of State; and eventually they will be brought within the national non-domestic rating system.

6   *Public Finance and Accountancy*, 19 May 1989.

7   The government argues that the tax base for the poll tax is the human beings living in each area: so, inasmuch as the new system takes account of population, it does equalise resources. However, if resources are seen as material resources — ie, income or wealth — then the new grant system ignores resources.

8   This figure — the notional poll tax required to fund spending at the level of needs assessed by central government — depends on the relationship between the aggregate amount of spending assessed as necessary by central government, the total amount of (revenue support) grant, and the total amount of income from the business rate. The nominal level of poll tax equals total spending needed, less income from grant, less income from the business rate, all divided by the adult population. Thus cuts in grant or the business rate poundage result in an increase in the nominal poll tax required to fund spending at the level of the needs assessment.

9   Although some increase in average domestic tax bills is likely in England and Wales in the first year, and has occurred in Scotland (see Chapter 9).

10 Precepting is unnecessary when there is only one tier of authority, as is the case with the Scottish island councils.

11 *Family Expenditure Survey 1986*, published 1988.

12 Although its GDP per head is 95.1 per cent of the average, it scores third best on this measure (this is because so much industry and commerce is concentrated in one region — the South East — that the average is distorted).

13 These three regions all score better than average on low income, unemployment and numbers in receipt of benefits. The South West has GDP per head significantly below the average, while East Anglia is almost at the average, and the South East considerably above it.

14 The Scottish figure is based on the actual amounts charged in 1989/90, with a deduction for water rates (see notes to the table for an explanation), whereas the other figures are government projections. This means that the English and Welsh figures are probably significantly underestimated on average — this turned out to be the case for government figures relating to Scotland, as we describe in the next chapter.

9 Deprivation and the poll tax

Scotland has been the testing ground for the poll tax. Here we extend the analysis of deprivation to look at the actual experience of the poll tax in Scotland. We then focus on how particular authorities in England are likely to be affected.

The Scottish experience

In order to analyse the effects of the poll tax on deprived areas, we ranked Scottish authorities on the basis of 'deprivation scores' from Scottish Office data.[1] The deprivation scores are based on three categories: socio-demographic (such as the number of one-parent households); economic, for example unemployment; and housing. The work was based on the 1981 census, which means that it unfortunately does not take account of subsequent changes. Nevertheless, the analysis appears to be sufficiently accurate for our purposes. It shows an extraordinary degree of concentrated deprivation.

We divide the Scottish authorities into three classes: those which are most deprived (nine authorities), a second grouping which are less deprived (20 authorities), and then the non-deprived authorities (27 authorities). (See note 2 for a detailed explanation of how we ranked the authorities.) Three words of caution are required. Firstly, poverty and deprivation are 'patchy'; the fact that an authority does not appear on a list as having above-average deprivation does not indicate the absence of poverty and deprivation within its borders. Secondly, the comparison is applied relative to a Scottish average; yet we have already seen that Scotland is generally more deprived than some English regions. So many of the apparently 'non-deprived' Scottish authorities might show up as deprived if compared with English authorities. Finally, the indicators seek to measure deprivation, not affluence. It would be wrong to assume that an absence of deprivation indicators implies above-average wealth or income.

Scottish poll tax levels

The introduction of the poll tax in Scotland from April 1989 gives us the first opportunity to compare the *actual* poll taxes charged both with the rates and with the government's projections of poll tax levels. The first conclusion to be drawn is that the increase in the average tax payment per adult has far outstripped both inflation and the predicted growth in national income. The average poll tax payment per adult in Scotland in 1989/90 is £301 (including water charges), 13 per cent above the average rate per adult of £266 in 1988/89 (including water rates).[3]

This substantial increase in real terms has occurred despite action by the government to try and keep poll tax levels as low as possible. Revenue Support Grant was increased by over 9 per cent — significantly above the rate of inflation. A change was made to the rules regarding local authority pension funds: for the next two years the index-linking of pensions can be financed by surpluses within the pension funds, rather than being a call on poll tax revenue.[4]

The reasons for this real increase in the level of local domestic taxes are complex. It is hard to disentangle those factors which are attributable directly to the abolition of domestic rates. Nevertheless, it is clear that such factors are at least partially responsible. Scottish authorities have had to allow for a higher proportion of revenue being lost through non-collection (generally 4.5 per cent) than was the case with rates. The increase in the business rate was capped at a level (of 5.9 per cent) which was significantly below the actual rise in costs faced by some local authorities. Central government has also consistently underestimated the costs of administration associated with the poll tax. There may be an element of authorities seeking to raise additional revenue in the first year of the poll tax to safeguard against the loss of safety nets in future years, but this is hard to gauge. There have also been additional pressures on local authority expenditure for reasons relating to other central government policies (such as its educational reforms).[5]

For these reasons, the government projections of poll tax levels have also proved to be significantly underestimated. The Scottish Office had assumed that the introduction of the poll tax would be 'revenue neutral'; the projected average poll tax for 1988/89 was £266 — the same as the average rate per adult. Had this figure gone up in line with the rise in prices, the average poll tax would have been £286 in 1989/90 — whereas the real figure is £301. If we consider the two amounts net of water charges (which makes them directly comparable with England and Wales), then the increase in local tax bills in excess of inflation has been over 6 per cent.

These figures lend support to our view that the method we adopted in Chapters 6 and 7 (when we looked at gainers and losers under the poll tax) was extremely cautious. We assumed a much lower real increase in average tax bills than has actually occurred in Scotland. They also lend support to critics of government projections of poll tax levels in England and Wales, who have always argued that these projections, like the Scottish ones, are underestimated.

Deprived authorities in Scotland

Table 9.1 shows the average poll tax levels for authorities grouped according to their degree of deprivation. We have calculated the level °of poll tax which would have been levied in each area without safety nets. Appendix 1 contains the average poll tax levels and deprivation ratios for individual Scottish authorities.

Table 9.1: Average Scottish poll tax levels by deprivation

Authority	Average poll tax levels (1989/90)
Most deprived	£331
Deprived	£306
Non-deprived	£261

Note: These are poll tax levels with the effect of safety nets eliminated. They include water charges.

There is a substantial gap between the average for the nine most deprived authorities and that for those authorities (around half) in the non-deprived category: the difference is £70 for an adult, or £140 for a couple. Six of the nine most deprived authorities have implied poll tax levels above the Scottish average of £301 (see Appendix 1).

These considerable differences between poll tax levels, to the detriment of deprived areas, do not simply reflect past differences between the levels of local taxation. Table 9.2 shows that rather than simply continuing to pay more in local taxation, residents in deprived areas are losing substantial amounts under the new structure.

Table 9.2: Average annual gains and losses per adult in Scotland

Area of residence (local authority area)	Average gains and losses per adult
Most deprived	- £35
Deprived	- £13
Non-deprived	£6

Note: Average poll tax levels (1989/90) are calculated with the effects of safety nets eliminated, and then deflated to 1988/89 prices (by a factor of 7.5%).

The 29 authorities which are classified as deprived on the Scottish Office data lose on average, while the 27 non-deprived authorities gain. The losses in the most deprived authority average £34 per adult.

These results reinforce the conclusion of our regional analysis: the new financial system introduced alongside the poll tax is leading to a substantial redistribution of resources away from highly deprived areas to more affluent ones. Moreover, in Scotland, the new tax has led to a substantial average loss for local taxpayers. We saw in Chapter 6 that the effect of the poll tax on different income groups is such that on average only top income earners are likely to have escaped the adverse effect of this increase in taxation.

Deprivation in England

Given the much larger number of authorities in England, we decided to focus our analysis by concentrating on two samples of 50 authorities each. These samples were selected on the basis of a Department of the Environment ranking of authorities by deprivation, employing indicators of a sort similar to those used by the Scottish Office in the work described above.[6] (Appendices 2 and 3 contain the deprived and non-deprived authorities with their deprivation ratio and poll tax level.)

How much to pay?

There is a projected gap of £96 between the average poll tax payable in deprived areas and that payable in non-deprived areas. According to these figures, taxpayers living in authorities with high deprivation will be liable for an average of £316 per person, compared to an average of £220 for residents in non-deprived authorities. For a couple, the averages are £632 and £440 respectively.

These averages, along with the rest of the analysis which follows, are based on Department of the Environment projections (without safety nets). If the Scottish experience is repeated in England and Wales, they probably underestimate the actual poll taxes which would be required even to fund current expenditure. Arguably, poll tax levels may be even higher in deprived authorities because the problem of evasion and non-collection is likely to hit deprived authorities worst, but we ignore that possibility in our analysis.

Averages can conceal considerable variations, and figure 9.1 illustrates the extent of variation by showing the number of authorities from each group whose projected poll tax levels fall within each range. The graph shows that there is indeed significant variation: ten of the 12 Inner London boroughs have projected poll taxes above £396. However, figure 9.1 shows that it is not simply Inner London which is responsible for the fact that deprived authorities will have significantly higher poll taxes. Up to the level of the projected average English poll tax of £246 per person,[7] non-deprived authorities outnumber deprived ones in each range. Indeed, four-fifths of the non-deprived authorities have poll taxes below the average, compared to less than a quarter of the deprived areas. When we look at the ranges above the average of £246, we see that deprived authorities start to predominate. Indeed, there is only one non-deprived authority with a projected poll tax level above the average level for deprived authorities (£316).

Figure 9.1 Poll tax levels in deprived and non-deprived authorities (England 1988/89)

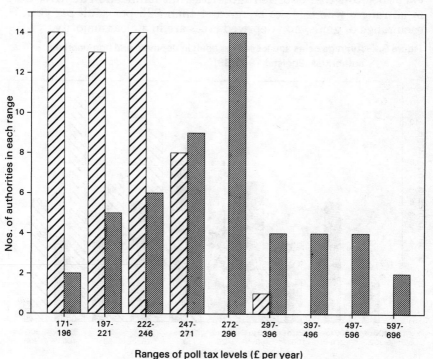

Note: Based on Department of Environment projection of poll tax levels, 1988/89. There are 50 authorities in each sample. The ranges of poll tax levels shown are of different sizes.

Source: Authors' calculations.

Gains and losses

The clear differences between the projected poll tax in deprived and non-deprived authorities do not simply reflect existing differences in the current levels of rates. The average rate bills are remarkably close in the two sets of authorities — in the non-deprived authority areas the average rate is £252 per adult (1988/89 levels), whereas in the deprived areas it is £256. Instead, these differences must be attributed to the changes in the financial system.

Overall, the average loss for each adult living in one of the deprived areas is £58 a year: their counterparts in non-deprived areas gain an average of £32 a year. Seventy per cent of the deprived authorities lose compared to 32 per cent of the non-deprived authorities. Figure 9.2 also shows that deprived authorities outnumber non-deprived ones in all ranges where losses are greater than £25 per adult per year. In each range of gains, non-deprived areas are in a clear majority.

Figure 9.2   Average gains and losses per adult in deprived and non-deprived authorities (England 1988/89)

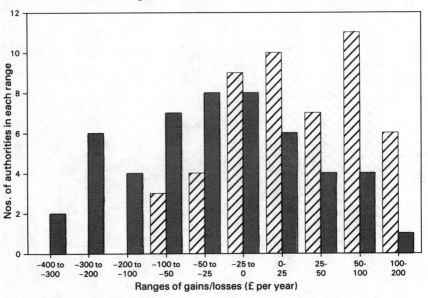

Non-deprived authorities   Deprived authorities

Note: Based on Department of Environment projection of poll tax levels, 1988/89. There are 50 authorities in each sample.
Source: Authors' calculations

These losses of revenue for deprived authorities will be phased in over the four-year period during which safety nets will apply. During that period, those authorities which lose will have either to increase the poll tax annually to cover the loss of revenue, or reduce net spending on services, or both.

Funding services

In the last chapter we described the problem of 'gearing' whereby increases in spending or changes in government grant have a disproportionate effect on poll tax levels. Here we examine the effects of 'gearing' on the two samples of English authorities. The problem of gearing bears particularly heavily on deprived authorities. This is because their need to spend is greater — so a proportionate increase in spending is likely to involve a higher cash increase. Our analysis shows that although the 'gearing' effect is severe for all of the 100 authorities in our two groupings, the effects are almost universally worse for deprived authorities than for non-deprived authorities.

In order to test the different effects of gearing on the two sets of authorities, we calculated the poll tax required in each authority to fund spending at a level of 5 per cent above central government's needs assessment. All of the 100 local authorities would require an increase in the poll tax of at least 13 per cent in order to fund this level of spending: the poll tax would have to rise from the £202 figure to at least £229. This illustrates how the problem of gearing afflicts *all* authorities which want to fund improvements in services, rich or poor.

However, there are clear differences between the two groups of authorities (see figure 9.3). Increases in the non-deprived authorities to fund a 5 per cent improvement in services are clustered around the average for the group of 15.4 per cent (equal to an increase in the poll tax from £202 to £233). Indeed, all 50 of these authorities have poll tax increases falling in the range 13.0 per cent to 17.5 per cent. On the other hand, 42 of the 50 deprived authorities would require poll tax increases to fund this level of services of above 17.5 per cent, and the average increase required by these authorities would be 21.7 per cent (equal to an increase in the poll tax from £202 to £246).

We have described these gearing effects in terms of increased spending, but it is important to recognise that exactly the same effects occur as a result of changes to the central government needs assessments. A 5 per cent cut in the needs assessment for deprived authorities would on average cause poll taxes to go up by 21.7 per cent, while in non-deprived authorities the average increase would be 15.4 per cent. Increases in central government needs assessments would have the converse effect — average cuts in poll taxes of 21.7 per cent and 15.4 per cent.[8]

In summary, the new financial system is designed to provide equity between authorities as long as they conform with the spending assessments laid down by central government. As soon as an authority strays above this level, the penalty on its poll tax payers is harsh. What we have shown here is that the penalty will tend to be harsher still for

Figure 9.3 The problem of 'gearing': Poll tax increase required to fund a spending level 5% above central government needs assessment (GREA) in deprived and non-deprived authorities (England 1988/89)

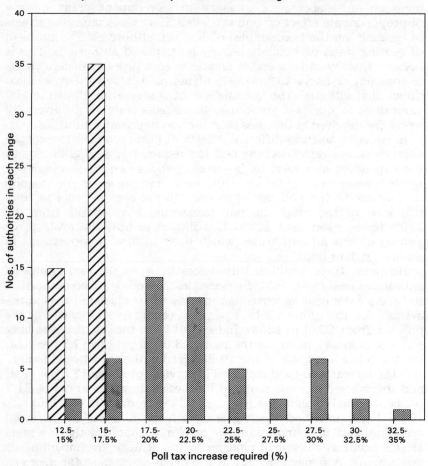

Non-deprived authorities   Deprived authorities

Note: Based on Department of the Environment projection of poll tax levels, 1988/89 and needs assessments for 1988/89. The increases are those required to increase spending 5% above the level of spending assessed as necessary by central government, rather than those required to increase spending above the actual current level. Thus, local authorities are compared on a standard basis, ignoring the effects of local spending decisions. There are 50 authorities in each sample.

Source: Authors' calculations

those with the misfortune to live in areas of high deprivation. Where the needs are greatest, the burden of taxation imposed by service improvements will also be greatest. Moreover, the effects of variations in central government needs assessments will be equally severe.

Conclusion

In this chapter we have found that in Scotland it is authorities with high deprivation which stand to have the highest poll taxes when the transitional protection of safety nets is withdrawn, and which stand to lose most under the new financial regime. In England we found this pattern repeated, but we also took the analysis a stage further: here we demonstrated that, if voters in deprived areas choose service provision slightly above the level assessed as necessary by central government, they face an even harsher penalty than that meted out to residents in non-deprived areas.

In both cases, these losses in deprived areas are to be phased in over a transitional period. During that period, deprived authorities which spend at a constant level will have to impose large annual increases in the poll tax. The only alternative will be to offset some or all of the lost revenue through cutting net expenditure on services.

Overall, the poll tax seems likely to make deprivation worse. This is partly because, as we saw in Chapters 6 and 7, it will make the majority of the poor worse off. But it is also because it will hit deprived areas hardest, and will make the improvement of public services most difficult precisely where needs are most acute.

Notes

1 George Duguid and Richard Grant, *Areas of Special Need in Scotland*, Scottish Office Central Research Unit.

2 We calculated our 'deprivation ratio' for Scottish authorities as follows. The authors of the Scottish Office study list for each authority its proportion of the most deprived enumeration districts (a term used to describe small geographical areas used in the 1981 census) in Scotland (ie, those falling into the worst 10 per cent), and its proportion of all enumeration districts, deprived or non-deprived. Our ratio is simply the proportion of deprived districts divided by the proportion of all districts. So a ratio of 1 would indicate an exactly proportionate share of deprived enumeration districts; a ratio greater than 1 shows a larger than proportionate share of such districts; and a ratio of zero shows that the authority has no highly deprived enumeration districts.

On this basis we placed nine authorities in the most deprived category — these are authorities with a deprivation ratio of more than 1, which means they each include a disproportionately large number of very deprived enumeration districts. The second group covers the next 20 authorities — those with a ratio between 0.25 and 0.96: these authorities include a significant number of deprived areas. The third category is the 27 authorities with the lowest proportions of deprived enumeration districts (ratios vary from 0 to 0.24).

3 This average is calculated on the basis of adjusted population figures used by

the Scottish Office in calculating the distribution of Revenue Support Grant. These figures ignore adults who are exempt, but include an allowance for standard community charge payments on empty properties.

4   *Public Finance and Accountancy*, 3 February 1989.

5   There are a number of other more technical reasons for the rise in local authority costs. Authorities have had to recoup money lost as a result of grant penalties imposed by central government in 1988/89; and in that year extensive use was made of balances to finance expenditure — in 1989/90 that spending is falling on the poll tax payer. Rating appeals have reduced revenue from the rates to an unexpected extent, causing a loss of revenue which again has to be recouped. The government's expenditure assumptions did not take full account of additional costs falling on local government: such as the costs of police and fire service pay awards, new standards for the staffing of schools, etc. For a fuller explanation of these issues see: Convention of Scottish Local Authorities, *Revenue Support Grant (Scotland) Order 1988 and Rate Support Grant (Scotland) (No 2) Order 1988 — observations by the Convention of Scottish Local Authorities on the above orders*, 9 January 1989.

6   The Department of the Environment has calculated indicators of deprivation in local authority areas — known as z-scores. These are standardised scores which provide a single index of deprivation based on the percentage of: unemployed persons, overcrowded households, single parent households, households lacking exclusive use of basic amenities, pensioners living alone and residents living in households where the head of household was born in the New Commonwealth or Pakistan. Areas with above-average deprivation have a positive score and areas with below-average deprivation have a negative score. The size of the score depends on the extent to which an area is above or below the average. The 50 authorities which we rank as the most deprived range from 6.69 to 1.60, and the 50 authorities which we rank as the least deprived range from -4.39 to -2.84. (Information Note No 2, *Urban Deprivation*, Department of the Environment.) We excluded the City of London because of the special legislative arrangements which apply there. Welsh authorities were also excluded because they are subject to a separate grant regime. As in the Scottish case, we do not place any weight in our analysis on the particular ranking of individual authorities, in case they are affected either by changes since the last census or by the weights given to particular indicators. For the same reason we do not assume that the sample of 50 deprived authorities is necessarily an exclusive list of all the most deprived areas in England. However, the sample contains many of the most deprived areas, and as a class our sample of deprived authorities is very substantially more deprived than our sample of non-deprived authorities. The two samples therefore provide a sound basis for comparing the impact the poll tax is likely to have on deprived and non-deprived areas. Moreover, they have a further advantage: coming from the Department of the Environment, these deprivation indicators could have been used by civil servants when advising ministers about the effects of replacing the rates with the poll tax, had ministers been concerned about the impact on deprivation.

7   Department of the Environment figures for 1988/89 without safety nets.

8   These increases and decreases are calculated in relation to the standard amount of poll tax calculated by central government as necessary to fund spending at the needs assessment level (not the poll tax required to fund actual current spending).

10 More power to individuals

In this chapter we discuss a key aspect of the government's case for its social security and local government finance policies: the assertion that recent legislation changes are strengthening individual rights and giving people more power over their own lives.

The right to vote and the poll tax register

John Selwyn Gummer is quite clear that the poll tax will not deter the exercise of democratic rights:

> The community charge is not a tax on voting. It is a charge for the use of local authority services which has nothing whatever to do with the right to vote. The community charge register and the electoral register will be compiled separately, will be maintained separately and will have rather different coverage.[1]

However, the government's legislation gives the officer responsible for the poll tax register (the Community Charge Registration Officer, or CCRO) explicit powers to use the electoral register. As an example of how this will work in practice, consider the description in *Public Finance and Accountancy* of the computer programme which is being used to compile the poll tax register in Rotherham:

> The programme will operate on the basis of reading every electoral record, matching it with the address on the rates or rent files and comparing it with the surname on the rates file for private properties and the rents file for local authority-owned properties. If surnames agree *only the electoral record* will be posted to the accounts file of the IRS (Initial Registration System), otherwise all names from both the rates or the rent files together with the electoral record will be posted.[2]

It is plain that in this authority the electoral register will be the primary source of initial information for the CCRO. The Department of the Environment suggests that the CCRO cross-check data from the initial canvass against the electoral register.[3] Efficient registration is seen as involving complete computerised interchange between the two systems.

It is perfectly true to say that the tax is not based on the act of voting itself. It is equally true that those who enter their names on the electoral register become known — in most cases immediately — to the CCRO, who requires them to register for the poll tax if they have not already done so.

If they refuse to comply, they are liable for a penalty of £50 in the first instance, followed by further penalties of £200 repeated until they agree to register. These penalties are imposed at the discretion of the CCRO, without a court hearing. Once they have been imposed, the offender may appeal. It was estimated that in Scotland at least £240,000 worth of these penalties had been levied by 1 April 1989.[4] The CCRO for Fife regional council pointed out that, among 4,000 people who faced penalties, there were 'a good few hundred' elderly people who were simply confused. Under the legislation, an exemption applies to people who are mentally handicapped as the result of a congenital disease or injury: it does not apply to those who become confused as a result of a degenerative disease. James Thompson said:

> I can offer these people nothing at all — we made a case for them a long time ago but the community charge is simply an indiscriminate tax.[5]

Because the poor are hit hardest by the poll tax and may in many cases be driven to desperation by the tax, it is they who are most likely to be tempted to give up their right to vote in the hope of evading the tax. But only those who also surrender their other claims on local welfare services will stand any chance of successfully evading the poll tax. The legislation gives the CCRO the right to acquire lists of names and addresses of people in contact with any other department of the local authority — including social services — with the exception of payroll and police records. Those who attempt non-registration will in practice be unable to take a council tenancy, claim housing benefit, use council leisure services, or go to a social worker. Nor will they be able to claim income support, as the Department of Social Security (DSS) will pass the names of its clients on to CCROs.

In reality, those who will be tempted to go 'unofficial' in this way are those who do not yet have a relationship with local welfare services — the young, casually employed or unemployed without a place of their own. The consequence may be that a large number of this group may simply opt out of official society.

Indeed, there is evidence that this is already happening. In Scotland, the number of people on the electoral register has dropped by around 26,000.[6] It is estimated that only a third of this fall in registration is due to population changes; the rest is due to people attempting to avoid paying the poll tax. Those who have 'disappeared' from the official register are frequently young people, just about to reach voting age. Electoral registration has fallen most significantly — up to 15 per cent — in the poorest housing estates. This pattern is not confined to Scotland. A survey of inner city local authorities in London has shown an unexpected drop in registration on the electoral roll of close to 28,000 people.[7] This may be due to fears of the introduction of the poll tax.

Confidentiality

Avoidance is only one of the many problems associated with the registration process. Registration is dependent on a systematic breaching of the confidentiality of highly sensitive welfare services. Already, the take-up of means-tested benefits, including housing benefit, is very low: undoubtedly this is in part to do with the fear of stigma, and of being dependent on what can be an intrusive bureaucracy. The same concerns often apply more strongly to contact with social workers. This fear is likely to be strengthened by the fact that personal information is now available to a department which has nothing to do with the provision of the service being taken up. The problem is illustrated by the description of preparations for registration in Rotherham. There, the view is that the pattern of exchanging information between departments 'must eventually develop into permanent bonds for the cross-flow of information as well as breaking down inter-departmental/sectional barriers'.[8]

Elected members may well intervene to prevent this disregard for confidentiality from developing in the way envisaged above. However, they are hamstrung by the legislation. They have a duty to ensure that the poll tax is collected efficiently; and, although they can prevent direct access to personal files by computer, they are obliged to hand names and addresses over to the CCRO — who has independent statutory powers — if requested to do so in writing. Thus the fundamental principle of confidentiality cannot be effectively defended by local authorities within the law.

It is the poor who will mainly suffer from these assaults on confidentiality: it is they who are more likely to depend on housing benefit than mortgage interest tax relief (Inland Revenue files are not open to CCROs); more likely to be council tenants than owner-occupiers; more likely to have contact with social workers; more likely to have their children in state schools (and therefore be known to the local education authority). The message is clear: those who use state services cannot expect the same standards of privacy as would be expected from the private sector.

The new bureaucracy

As we have seen, the poll tax comes with a range of fierce enforcement powers vested in local authorities. Although many authorities will no doubt attempt to apply a sympathetic policy to the problems of those who cannot afford the tax, they will also be governed by the imperative of revenue collection. There is a risk of the relationship between local authorities and poor people becoming soured. The local authority may apply to the DSS to have poll tax arrears deducted from income support, or to employers for deductions from earnings. For those (such as people on invalidity pensions) not in work or on income support, there is the prospect of seizure of their personal possessions or (in England and Wales) imprisonment.

For those who receive income support, deductions for arrears of poll tax may come on top of several other deductions — for fuel arrears, social fund loans or rent arrears. In combination, these deductions will deprive claimants of control over much of their income, as the following example shows:

> One pregnant lone parent with three children under five was described by a duty social worker as destitute. Her [benefit] of £75.50 [per week] was reduced by £26.93 because of electricity and gas direct payments and deductions for two outstanding social fund loans which she received for a cooker and maternity clothes.[9]

If claimants on income support already have a high level of existing debt, the local authority may decide to waive its right to make direct deductions and opt to try to seize personal possessions.

The collection process, in combination with the registration process, involves a massive increase in bureaucracy. It is estimated that the volume of correspondence involved in tax collection will triple in England and Wales, excluding monthly letters to those in arrears.[10] The volume of payments made is also likely to increase dramatically. For example, Rochdale council estimates that it will receive 1.75 million poll tax payments annually, compared with 0.38 million rate receipts. Several authorities are installing protective screens in offices where the poll tax will be paid: this is perhaps symbolic of the actual effect the poll tax will have on the relationship between local authorities and the public. The inevitable growth of bureaucracy increases the likelihood of errors and confusion. This has certainly been the case in Scotland. It may well be that the poll tax, far from bringing residents greater independence, will enmesh them in a tangle of an ever more complicated bureaucracy.

Joint and several liability

The joint and several liability provisions appear to undermine the government's case that accountability depends on an individual tax. The tax is not legally an individual one as far as married and cohabiting couples are concerned. If the objective is to provide each individual with their own *bill* rather than to enforce individual *liability*, then sending the spouses of householders a copy of the rates bill would have been as effective.

Moreover, that would have avoided another intrusive aspect of poll tax administration — the enforcement of the cohabitation rule. This is the rule under which a judgement is made as to whether two single people should be considered to be 'living together as man and wife'. The cohabitation rule has been one of the provisions in the social security system which has caused the most resentment and tension, and there is no reason for optimism that it will operate better in relation to the poll tax, particularly as there is no right of appeal to a tribunal — the first judicial consideration of the decision is at the magistrates' court.

According to government guidelines, local authorities have the power to enforce joint and several liability when arrears have accrued. Although there should be no need for local authorities to seek information about the nature of personal relationships until a couple falls into debt, some local authorities have been asking for this type of information on the registration forms.[11] Nevertheless, it will be poorer couples, more likely to fall into arrears, who will be at greater risk of experiencing the intrusive cohabitation rule.

Of course, had the rebates system been reformed to match the intent of the poll tax, then individual liability for the poll tax could have been retained. For the logic of an individual tax is that there should be *individually* assessed rebates to match. It was only the prospect of married and cohabiting women who would simply not have an income from which the poll tax could be paid, and who would not be entitled to rebates, which forced the government to adopt a peculiar hybrid solution: an *individual* tax levied on the basis of *joint* liability, with rebates assessed on *family* income.

Yet this hybrid leaves women in couples in a particularly vulnerable position, and not just in relation to the intrusiveness of checks on personal relationships.[12] While a woman is living with a man, she will have no eligibility for a rebate, unless both their incomes are very low. Thus she may have no means whatsoever of paying her poll tax. Yet liability will accrue not just for her own tax, but for her partner's as well. If they subsequently divorce or separate, she may be held liable for paying off the arrears of *both* bills. Although local authorities are encouraged to seek to enforce the debt against the partner who was earning during the period of the relationship, in practice it may only be possible to pursue the partner who remains in the marital home — usually the woman. Even though she may have given up paid employment in order to look after children, she could be held liable to pay not just her own poll tax but that of her ex-husband too. Very often, on divorce or separation, a woman's income drops. So it may well be that women on low incomes following separation will have to pay arrears accrued when the family income was higher.

Local discretion: the social fund

We saw in Chapter 3 how the government has justified its social security reforms as involving a greater degree of independence for individuals. Yet, because dependence has been associated with state provision and independence with private provision, the government has failed to focus on the *actual* effects of the changes to state benefits on claimants. Here we consider three examples of the reforms, to demonstrate that the subject is rather more complicated than the simple distinction between state and private provision allows.

The social fund involves the replacement of a legal entitlement with bureaucratic discretion. Previously, grants for exceptional need were payable under statutory regulations, with a right of appeal to an independent tribunal. Instead, the social fund provides discretionary payments, usually in the form of a loan; the only form of redress for an aggrieved claimant is an internal review carried out by social fund officers themselves, with final resort to the social fund inspector, who is paid by the DSS but nominally independent.

Results from a survey of social services departments show that social fund officers have tended to treat DSS guidance as though it has the force of law — which it does not. But the discretionary decisions taken by these officials cannot be challenged by an appeal.[13] Moreover, claimants have been put off making applications for a number of reasons. A survey by the National Association of Citizens' Advice Bureaux (NACAB) in the early stages of the new scheme found that:

> Of the cases where an application had not yet been made ... 45 per cent were going to proceed with an application... Only 29 per cent were not applying because they were ineligible. The main reason for not applying was reluctance (68 per cent); clients did not want a loan, were concerned by the high rates of repayment and were put off by the process of claiming a social fund payment.[14]

The law requires social fund officers to consider the availability of help from another person or organisation before making a payment.

This is consistent with the government's view that assistance provided independently of the state is preferable, because it removes the claimant from a relationship of dependency on state provision. But claimants themselves do not necessarily agree with this simple distinction between dependence and independence. For instance, in a study of mothers' experiences in claiming social fund payments, Ruth Cohen found:

> Help from friends, neighbours and relatives could be seen as preferable to reliance on the state, but it is clear that mothers usually do not see it in this way. They speak of feeling guilty or degraded, or accepting gifts as a last resort. It seems that they are forced into asking for help, or that relatives or friends, often poor themselves, may feel obliged to fill the gap for the sake of the baby.[15]

The social fund involves a loss of rights both for those who claim and for those who do not. Those who claim place themselves in a position of dependency on the discretionary judgement of an official: they have no legal means of redress if that discretion is exercised unfairly. Those who do not claim are excluded from access to provision for needs which were previously recognised as essential. They must either do without or accept a relationship of dependency on friends, relations or charities: to them this may be far more demeaning than claiming a state benefit provided as of right.

Charity

Similar objections can be made to the other arm of the government's policy for meeting those needs which fall outside the compass of weekly state benefits: charity. The Social Security Act 1986 established the 'Independent Living Fund' to be run by a body of trustees appointed by the government, with the assistance of the Disablement Income Group (a charity). The fund gives out grants on a discretionary basis to severely disabled people who lost out as a result of the April 1988 social security changes. A similar approach was adopted after an error in the calculation of the retail price index resulted in considerable losses for many claimants. The government compensated some groups of claimants directly, but the needs of other groups were nominally dealt with by giving over £7 million to charities to distribute.

The government perceives an important role for charity, as a substitute for parts of state provision:

> We now need to extend this spirit of [self help] further into the areas called the 'welfare state'. There are optimistic signs that this is happening

already... [one good example is] the strong growth in voluntary giving to independent charities.[16]

However, there is little indication that charitable giving is increasing sufficiently to be able to take over responsibilities from the welfare state and discharge them adequately. The Charities Aid Foundation estimates that personal giving is running at only £1.5 billion a year, less than 1 per cent of personal disposable income. Since 1975, the value of charitable donations has failed to keep pace with the increase in earnings (there has been an increase of less than 2 per cent above the rate of inflation). Moreover, because of the nature of different charities (from private schools to rifle clubs to the alleviation of poverty), the rich gain as much as the poor from the overall work of the charitable sector.[17]

A more fundamental point concerns the desirability of substituting charity for state provision. The distinctive aspect of charity is that it is voluntary for givers, and uncertain for recipients. Those who depend on charity must surrender their independence and rely on the generosity of donors and the good judgement of officials who dispense the aid. Government arguments in favour of charity concentrate on the advantages to taxpayers — financially and morally — of paying their money voluntarily to charity rather than compulsorily to the state. As Michael Prowse wrote in the *Financial Times*:

> The government has so far concentrated on the moral superiority of giving; but what it should be asking is what kind of welfare best serves the needs of the unfortunate recipients of aid. The state as provider still has much to offer.[18]

The effect of the government's argument is to distract attention from the people who should surely be at the centre of welfare policy: those in need.

School meals

A slightly different perspective on the questions of choice and independence is provided by consideration of the government's policy on free school meals. Here the argument is more complex, with the government advocating the substitution of a cash benefit for payment in kind, rather than the simple curtailment of state provision. Under the Social Security Act 1986, local education authorities (LEAs) can only provide free meals for children in families on income support. Parents on family credit receive a notional cash compensation in their benefit for loss of entitlement to free school meals. Moreover, LEAs have lost their discretionary power to provide free meals for children whose families are not receiving income support but have a low income.

In its Green Paper, the government has justified the change of policy on the following basis:

> The government [has] concluded that so far as possible assistance should be provided by means of cash rather than benefits in kind. [It has] therefore decided not to extend the availability of free school meals and welfare foods to families receiving family credit... The school meal service has an important role to play but the extension of free school meals to a wider range of children is undesirable *in principle*. A substantial proportion of those entitled to benefits in kind do not take advantage of them and the Government believes it is better to give the families concerned adequate resources and the *freedom to choose* how to use them.[19] *(our emphasis)*

This purported objective of 'greater choice' depends on the adequacy of the compensation received by parents. Yet for many of those who claim family credit, the compensation (which is equivalent in 1989/90 to a weekly payment of £3.65 during term-time) does not meet the cost of school meals. Those who also claim housing benefit find that some of their compensation is clawed back: in the case of a tenant, at least £2.92 of the £3.65 compensation is deducted from their housing benefit.[20] Of course, the compensation is of no value to those who do not take up family credit. As we have seen, the take-up of family credit is very low—considerably lower than the 'substantial proportion' who the government said did not take up their free school meals.

The government's policy in this area does not address the important question of who should control what children eat at school meal times. It could be any combination of the following: central government (through nutritional standards for school meals, abolished in 1980); local education authorities; schools; parents; children. For many parents, the increased 'choice' provided by cash is largely fictitious. Although parents may receive some additional cash, they (usually women) are forced either to spend time preparing lunches themselves, or give the money to the child who then spends it as she or he sees fit. The 'extra choice' for parents turns out to be a choice between extra work or loss of control over their children's diets. Yet surely the government would agree that a child's diet is an appropriate area of parental control, to be exercised by parents themselves or by teachers acting in their place.

Cultivating dependency

The government rejects a social security system based on the desirability of insurance and universal benefits in preference to means-tested benefits. It argues that state benefits imply a culture of dependency, and that an improved system of means-tested benefits can play a central role in the state system.

Yet the evidence is that take-up of means-tested benefits is consistently lower than that of universal benefits. The April 1988 reforms do not appear to have improved the position. The government appears to have ignored the evidence that there is a real and crucial distinction between means-tested benefits and other state benefits: that the problems of stigma and feelings of dependency, as well as the complexity of the claiming process and the poverty trap, apply almost exclusively to means-tested benefits.

Beveridge recognised the 'strength of popular resistance to any kind of means test' long ago:

> This objection springs not so much from a desire to get everything for nothing, as from resentment at a provision which appears to penalise what people have come to regard as the duty and pleasure of thrift, of putting pennies away for a rainy day. Management of one's income is an essential element of a citizen's freedom.[21]

A reform process which seeks to empower claimants and strengthen their aspirations towards independence should surely put the preference of claimants themselves for universal benefits at the centre of its deliberations.

Moreover, the discussion of dependency and independence in relation to welfare ignores taxation. As our material on living standards showed (see Chapters 5 to 7), the reductions in taxation have been targeted on the better-off. Fiscal welfare is not seen by the government as state support and is therefore not treated by them as an example of 'dependency'. The Conservative Bow Group put the point very clearly:

> [the] debate ... on the dependency problem ... has started in a worryingly if not wholly surprisingly blinkered way. The images conjured up ... are those of the unmarried teenage mother in a council flat, the long-term unemployed industrial worker and his family: whereas a full account should include pictures of the middle class family drawing no welfare benefits or dole, but mortgaged up to their eyeballs.[22]

In formulating its social security policy, the government seems to have avoided a detailed analysis of the actual choices and relationships which structure claimants' lives. The assumption that less state provision would automatically bring about greater self-reliance and choice has masked the reality: in many instances policies have brought about greater dependency and less self-reliance.

The poll tax and accountability

There is a similar lack of regard for the practical effects of introducing the poll tax. The administration of the poll tax involves a substantial increase of bureaucracy, an erosion of civil liberties and a threat to the franchise. What then of the overriding objective which appears to have made all of this palatable to the government — the enhancement of accountability?

Our analysis has highlighted a number of problems. The government's notion of accountability seems to entail the imposition of financial discipline on voters, rather than the operation of structures within which they can exercise control over local authorities. If this is empowerment, then it is of an extremely selective type: power to those who wish to curtail local spending, but not for those who think differently.

The 'gearing effect' imposes a disproportionate penalty on voters who wish to elect for better services, as well as on authorities whose needs are underestimated by central government. Moreover, as our analysis in Chapter 9 showed, this effect strikes authorities in deprived areas with considerably greater ferocity than their more affluent neighbours.

A further distortion of financial accountability occurs because of the squeeze on local finances which is built into the new financial arrangements. The capping of increases in business rate income implies that the domestic sector will have to bear a greater share of taxation as time goes by. The only practical way of avoiding this is likely to be cuts in services.

For deprived authorities in particular this general problem is compounded by their huge losses as a result of the new financial system. This places a very substantial extra financial burden on their residents, who are in any case predominantly badly off and who suffer from the regressive nature of the poll tax. The phasing in of these losses over a three- to five-year period alleviates the immediate damage, but prolongs the agony. Each year during the transitional period, most deprived authorities must either raise the poll tax substantially in real terms, or cut net spending on services, or both.

The government appears to assume that the operation of local democracy has resulted in a higher level of services, and consequently of expenditure, than is justified by popular support. Central government action is required to adjust the balance in favour of lower expenditure and less direct provision by local authorities. Yet, if this argument is correct, then why is it necessary to weight the financial system to deter higher spending? Why not introduce a financial regime which allows local voters a more neutral choice between high or low spending? It seems that central government wishes to have it both ways: arguing that the key question for local democracy is how much to spend, but also wishing to retain centrally the power to influence the outcome strongly.

The government has suggested that the poll tax will bring in its wake a reduction in local authority services and thereby greater personal choice. But does less state provision of services bring greater freedom? Not so for the poor. As Chapter 1 showed, people on low incomes are far more reliant on welfare state services to supplement their incomes than the better-off. Moreover, they have fewer options: for example, a pensioner, already reliant on a state pension, is unlikely to be in a position to turn to private provision. Again, the theory doesn't address the reality of the lives of those who rely on state provision for their welfare.

Community charge?

The government believes that charges for services are preferable to taxes, because charges are equitable (you pay for what you get) and efficient (you get what you want). The idea is that, if local government services operated more on market lines, then the benefits of the market would accrue.

The poll tax is partly intended to lead to an increase in the use of specific charges for services. Indeed, the government is now introducing legislation which enables the Secretary of State to extend the scope of local authority charges for services. Increasing charges is one practical response to the squeeze on local finances brought about by the cap on business taxation and the highly regressive form of domestic taxation. Yet such charges may well reduce access to services for the poorest, and risk becoming a form of 'perverse targeting', whereby people most in need of services are deprived of access to them for want of money.

The government's argument also rests on the assertion that the new tax will be closer to a charge for services than the rates. Yet there appear to be two very basic fallacies on which this argument is based. Firstly, it is suggested that the poll tax is analogous to a charge, because it involves payment for a 'bundle of services' which every individual receives. However, there is no evidence to suggest that the poll tax *does* result in a payment proportionate to the use made of local services. Indeed, the little research that is available suggests that it does not even match the use made of services by different income or social groups — let alone the use made by each particular household, and by each individual within each household.[23]

The second fallacy rests on a confusion about the distinction between public services and market provision. The market relationship between charges and consumer satisfaction rests on the voluntary nature of the transaction. If the consumer dislikes the quality or price of the product, s/he can in theory select another product or not buy the product at all. In turn, this is supposed to impose discipline on producers to meet consumer demand at acceptable prices. None of this applies to local government taxation, except in the limited sense that people can migrate to get away from local authorities they dislike. Local authorities are elected by universal franchise to provide public services funded in part by compulsory taxation. It is illegal not to pay the 'community charge' — which is, of course, not true of buying goods in the market place. Voting for councillors periodically to set a budget for the overall level of spending on services cannot be equated with buying an individual product in the supermarket.

The distinctive character of public (as opposed to market) provision underlies both a strength and a weakness of local government. The strength is that, because public services need not rely on specific charges for services, communities can pool their resources and act together to provide services and resolve problems which the market is incapable of tackling. The weakness is that a form of accountability which relies on infrequent majority voting creates a risk of local authorities being unresponsive to the needs of those they serve. The government seems to recognise the necessity of local authorities providing some public services — and therefore, implicitly at least, to accept that the market cannot entirely supplant the role of local democracy. Yet, when it comes to the specific problems of accountability and responsiveness, the government appears to assume they can be spirited away by pretending that a local tax is a 'charge' and assuming that somehow the magic of the market will do the rest. The problems of making local authorities more responsive to the needs of their communities deserve more serious treatment than this.

Conclusion

The practical workings of the poll tax and some of the recent social security changes appear to have disabled rather than empowered. The bureaucracy and discretion associated with the social security reforms have reduced the rights of individual claimants and the ideal of greater choice has not been realised. The reform of local government finance fails to address seriously the task of making local authorities more responsive to the needs to individuals within their communities. Instead, the reform falls back on a bogus analogy between a flat-rate tax and market changes.

Certainly there are individuals and areas where power has been enhanced. Those on higher incomes have more money and more purchasing power. For the most part they live in non-deprived areas whose authorities can afford to sustain services and cut poll taxes, because of the windfall gains they receive under the new financial system. But these gains are part of a process of division which threatens to bring about a more fragmented community. Not only do some individuals and areas lose heavily, but some individuals may be pushed out of the democratic process altogether, choosing the loss of all rights in exchange for an escape from an intrusive and unfair tax.

If communities do become more fragmented in this way, it will not only be poorer individuals and areas which lose power. In addition, the capacity of communities to tackle problems and challenges in a cohesive fashion will also be eroded.

Notes

1   Speech by the Rt Hon John Selwyn Gummer MP at Blakeney, Norfolk, 7 October 1988.
2   John Wadsworth and David Morley, 'Compiling a register for the poll tax', *Public Finance & Accountancy*, 24 February 1989. Authors' original emphasis.
3   'The Community Charge: The Community Charges Register', Community Charge Practice Note No 3.
4   *Independent*, 1 April 1989.
5   James Thompson, Fife regional council CCRO, quoted in Norman James, *Community Charge: what it means for housing*, Institute of Housing in Scotland 1988.
6   *Independent*, 31 May 1989.
7   See note 6.
8   See note 2.
9   Quoted in J & G Stewart, 'Fund of badwill', *Community Care*, January 1989.
10 *Municipal Journal*, 10 March 1989.
11 *Observer*, 28 May 1989. The Data Protection Registrar has ruled that such questions are unlawful if the CCRO intends to store the information on computer. This is because it is not required for the purpose of *registration*.
12 The legal position of men and women is the same under joint and several liability; however, because women have less access to an income of their own, their position is more vulnerable than men's.
13 See note 9.
14 *The Social Security Act: First Impressions*, NACAB, November 1988.
15 R Cohen and M Tarpey, *Single Payments: the disappearing safety net*, CPAG Ltd 1988. This refers to payments made under the regulatory social fund.
16 Speech by the Rt Hon John Moore MP, 26 September 1987.
17 'A new dependence on charity', *Financial Times*, 31 October 1988.
18 See note 17.
19 *Reform of Social Security*, Green Paper, Vol 2, Cmnd 9518, HMSO 1985.
20 The £2.92 figure is for Scotland where 80 per cent of the compensation is withdrawn for a tenant (65 per cent taper for rent rebates and 15 per cent taper for poll tax rebates). For more information, see S McEvaddy, *One Good Meal a Day*, CPAG Ltd 1988.
21 Sir William Beveridge, *Social Insurance and Allied Services*, Cmnd 6404, p12.
22 *Crossbow*, journal of the Bow Group, autumn 1988.
23 Glen Bramley, Julian Le Grand and William Low, 'How far is the poll tax a "community charge"? The implications of service usage evidence', Discussion Paper, April 1989.

11   Local welfare in the 1990s

In this chapter, we draw together some of the threads of our argument and consider the policy questions raised by the analysis and evidence. We also suggest some alternative policies for local government finance and taxation.

A more divided community

Recent social security changes and the introduction of the poll tax have combined to shift resources from the poor to the rich. Low-income groups are worse off under the new social security and tax regimes than they would have been under the old system uprated in line with the growth in national income. Money has been redistributed from these groups to the better-off in large quantities.

This has taken place against a background of substantial local authority involvement in social security. Despite the general desire of central government to curtail the scope of local authority responsibilities, this involvement has not diminished in the 1980s — indeed, it has grown to a small extent. However, this has not meant that local authorities have had the powers to counter the divisive effects of the government's social security policies. As is illustrated by the sorry histories of housing benefit and free school meals, benefits administered by local authorities are a convenient target for government spending cuts. In some areas — such as housing benefit local schemes — discretionary powers to provide additional benefits over and above statutory entitlements have been curtailed. Meanwhile, there is a parallel process of introducing greater discretion under the rule of the cash limit, as a substitute for entitlements under the rule of law. The social fund is the key example of an attempt by central government to implicate local authorities in such a process; attempts to use the housing benefit subsidy system to compel authorities to restrict payments are based on similar principles.

The poll tax continues and accentuates the trend of redistribution from the poor to the better-off. In addition, it hits deprived areas hardest, placing the greatest burden on those communities with the greatest number of poor families, and rendering the funding of services hardest where needs are highest. Thus the poll tax is a threat to the services on which poorer families rely, as well as to their incomes.

As it becomes more difficult to fund services from general taxation, the pressure will grow for services to be funded by charges. In some cases, these charges may be levied by local authorities themselves, while in others the private sector may take over — especially where authorities are compelled to put services out to tender under recent privatisation legislation. In either case, the further intrusion of market principles will tend to exclude and pauperise low-income families. Either they will give up using services because they cannot afford them, or they will be compelled to cut their spending on other essentials in order to meet charges.

The poll tax promises greater divisions within communities. There is a real danger of encouraging the creation of a group which opts out of the democratic process altogether, by choosing to give up the right to vote and access to local services in the hope of evading the poll tax.

There is also the divisiveness which is inherent in the government's emphasis on the relationship between paying local taxes and benefiting from local services. The government assumes that, as well as paying an equal amount in taxation, each individual will derive an equal benefit from services. Yet in practice this is not true. The use of services varies between different income and social groups (and individuals within these groups). Strong feelings that poll tax levels should be reduced may be generated among those who pay a flat-rate 'charge' and feel that they do not derive sufficient personal benefit in return. Divisions between users and non-users of services may be emphasised, to the detriment of a debate about the proper level of local taxation based on a perception of the interest of the whole community in adequate public services.

At present, public perceptions focus on the unfairness of a tax which fails to mirror ability to pay. If the government's project succeeds and the idea of a flat-rate tax becomes rooted, the perception of unfairness may become inverted. It may be the failure of services to mirror a flat-rate tax — in other words, to deliver a similar volume and quality of services to each individual — which comes in for criticism, at least from those who use services less.

Both the recent social security changes and the poll tax clearly threaten a more divided community. We now turn to consider whether there are steps local authorities can take to resist this threat.

Serving the whole community

Local authorities need to focus on the relationship between paying taxation and benefiting from services. But they should not succumb to pressure to see this relationship in too narrow a way. Some services and activities are primarily of benefit to the whole community — planning controls are an obvious example. Others — such as street lighting — are arguably of more or less uniform benefit to all. Many others, such as expenditure on economic development, some invest- ment in roads, and expenditure on child protection and education, may give greater benefit to particular individuals or groups but are also services in which the whole community has an interest.

It would be a grave mistake to place a primary emphasis on, for example, the distributional consequences of child protection policies. It may be that these benefit children in low-income families to a greater extent than other children, but this is hardly an objective of the service. Local authorities need to be prepared to defend the notion of a community interest in objectives such as ensuring the safety of children and providing them with decent education. An obsession with the distributional consequences of policies could easily come to obscure this basic idea.

Prioritising services: who gains?

Nevertheless, in deciding what level of services to fund, the distribu- tional consequences will be of major significance. Local authorities should be especially concerned at the prospect of having to raise the poll tax in order to fund particular services which may be of greatest benefit to higher-income groups. In this context, the study of local authority services in Cheshire which we referred to in Chapter 1 is of interest (see box). Although it only analyses the services provided by one county council, it is an important indication of the way in which particular services are distributed.

Firstly, the overall picture offers some reassurance. The authors found that if rebates are taken into account, the share of services going to the poorest 20 per cent of households (the bottom quintile group) is slightly greater than the share of local taxation which they pay through the poll tax (see box).

Thus, although the poll tax is a regressive tax, on these figures it appears that it may not be so severely regressive as to eliminate a net average benefit to the poorest households from increased expenditure on local services.

But this is no cause for complacency. Low-income households can ill afford *any* decrease in their *cash* incomes. The fact that they may be receiving good value in terms of services is of little consolation if poll tax payments leave them without enough cash for food, clothing, fuel and so on. Moreover, if the average net benefit to the poorest households from increases in spending on services is generally as small as appears from these figures (see box), then a substantial minority of such households would in fact probably lose from such increases. Worse still, if the poll tax is increased to make up shortfalls in revenue from the business rate or grant, *all* such households would lose.

The Cheshire study: does local spending benefit the poor?[1]

The Cheshire study found that the proportion of services received by the lowest quintile group was slightly smaller than the share of net poll tax payments they were likely to have to meet. They received 16.1 per cent of the benefit derived from services, while it was estimated that they would pay between 11.2 per cent and 14.1 per cent of poll taxes, net of rebates.

Obviously some particular low-income households might lose from an increase of the poll tax to fund spending on services which they themselves do not use. But even these households are likely to be net beneficiaries from service provision overall — because of the contribution made to the funding of services by central government grant and the business rate.

The authors of the Cheshire study found that 16-plus and adult education, roads, country parks, libraries and waste tips were all used to a greater extent by the top quintile (20 per cent of households with the highest incomes) than by the bottom quintile. On the other hand, these services were of greater benefit to the bottom quintile: pre-16 education; other educational and youth services; all social service provision, including home helps, meals on wheels and services for the handicapped; and museums. Expenditure on public transport was found to be of approximately equal value to the top and bottom income groups.

There are also considerable differences in the use made of particular services by different income groups (see box). Where local authorities can gather this kind of information, it should be of immense help in taking the difficult budgetary decisions which will arise with the poll tax. Local authorities can use such information to prioritise service areas of particular benefit to the least well-off individuals and groups. They may wish, for example, to prioritise vocational training for manual occupations, or spending on parks in deprived areas.

Information on the distribution of services also enables an authority to identify an area of expenditure which is of greater benefit to more affluent families and to confront the question as to whether the community interest justifies it. Where such expenditure is incurred, local authorities should be looking to improve the access of less well-off families to these services. For example, it would be a mistake to cut back on expenditure on adult education simply if, as in Cheshire, take-up by poorer families is very low: better to examine the courses offered and see if they are relevant to the needs of these families, if they are encouraged to take up places, and so on.

Charging for services

There is a third option in addition to the alternatives of cutting services or increasing the poll tax — introducing or increasing charges for services. The government's Green Paper declared its intention of encouraging local authorities to charge for services wherever possible, and provisions in the Local Government and Housing Bill 1989 vastly extend the range of local services for which charges can be made.[2]

It should be plain from the analysis in this book that any assumption that charging can be made palatable by means-tested rebates is far from the truth. This approach runs the risk of stigmatising the poor and, linked with low take-up of means-tested rebates, could either reduce their incomes or their access to services. On the other hand, there may be services which are of disproportionate benefit to better-off households where charging is a sensible way of ensuring that those who can afford to pay do so. One measure which has been taken by councils which provide leisure facilities is to make higher charges for non-residents (who may come from more affluent areas with lower levels of public provision), while giving residents a card which entitles them to pay a lower amount.

This principle could be extended by using a discount card. For example, there could be variable rates of discount for those in work (least discount), pensioners, those on housing benefit, or income support (highest discount). Payment could be by subscription or by the advance purchase of units which would be cashed in for services (a system which is now being used for fuel pre-payment meters). The advantage of such a scheme would be that a card of this sort would be made available to all residents. This is one way of relating charges to ability to pay with a diminished problem of stigma. It is too early to judge the practicability or economic viability of these types of schemes. Their civil liberties aspects would need to be carefully considered. Moreover, charging is clearly inappropriate for services which primarily benefit the poor, or where it is an essential principle that they should be free at the point of access, such as advice services. Nevertheless, given the fact that local authorities have to rely on the regressive poll tax for revenue, discount schemes for some services are certainly worth investigation.

Responding to the poll tax: protecting the poor

In response to the poll tax, one of the main priorities of councils should be to identify any feasible measures which may offer some protection to those on low incomes. Given the nature of the poll tax, these measures are severely limited. Nevertheless, they are vitally important.

Rebates
Authorities need to give a high priority to good quality rebates administration, and to improved take-up of benefit. The additional caseload and administrative problems which result from the poll tax pose a challenge to local authorities probably on a greater scale than anything seen since the transfer of housing benefit in 1982/83. Yet it is easy for rebates to be seen as a side issue, given the mammoth task of compiling the poll tax register, setting up systems for billing and so on. This perception could be reinforced by the tendency for rebates administration to be absorbed within finance departments, on the basis that they are just one part of the overall poll tax operation.

The rebates service needs to be given a high status as a service to the public, rather than simply seen as part of the administration and collection of a tax. This is important so that potential applicants feel encouraged to take up their rebates, and so that staff have an ethos which emphasises *entitlement to benefits*, not *liability for a tax*. Moreover, if local authorities are to avoid the damaging administrative problems which particularly affected the early years of housing benefit, the proper resourcing of rebates administration is vital. It would be absurd for local authorities to complain about the inequality of the poll tax and then fail to process rebate applications speedily and accurately.

In addition, the poll tax brings a large number of people into entitlement to rebates for the first time who have no landlord to advise them on the scheme. Local authorities have to think imaginatively about how to contact such groups and advise them of entitlement. Although there is a cost to such take-up work, there is also a probable increase in revenue. Anyone entitled to a rebate is going to be in difficulty paying the poll tax unless they receive a rebate; and the rebate is almost entirely funded by central government. An authority which aims to register over 90 per cent of residents to pay a tax should also aim to register over 90 per cent of those entitled to receive a benefit.

Collection procedures
Collection procedures need to take full account of the fact that poverty will be the major reason for failure to pay the poll tax. Plainly authorities must collect the revenue on which services depend; but taking large numbers of court actions against people who cannot afford the tax is likely to prove costly and unproductive. Authorities must have procedures for checking entitlement to rebates and other

benefits, and for making welfare rights advice and debt counselling available. In some cases, this could involve the direct provision of information by collection staff to individuals in debt, in others it could mean referrals to advice agencies. In either case, the provision of this assistance must be seen as an integral part of collection policy, not an optional extra.

Joint and several liability
Authorities also need to consider their policies on joint and several liability. They are not obliged to follow the Department of Social Security's practice (in relation to the cohabitation rule), even though the government assumes that they will. Whether or not two people are living together in a quasi-marital relationship is a personal matter, and to elicit information about it requires great sensitivity. The skills required are more likely to be found in social service than in finance departments.[3] Rather than automatically adopting an intrusive approach based on investigation of private affairs, the starting point should be the individual's perception of their own relationship.

The worst problems are likely to arise where two people have been living in the same household, have fallen into arrears of poll tax, and now no longer live together. The temptation to try to collect from the woman just because she may have remained in the marital home should be strongly resisted. Where joint and several liability is established, and the couple are separated, authorities should make every effort to pursue the individual (usually the man) who had the higher income during the period of the relationship.

A code of confidentiality
Local authorities need a clear policy, perhaps in the form of a published code of practice, on privacy. As we have seen, the role of elected members is very limited, but they can reassure the public that they will not go beyond the requirements of the legislation in providing information to the Community Charge Registration Officer (CCRO). They can also seek assurances from the CCRO that s/he will not seek access to sensitive information such as names and addresses held by social workers or advice centres. Such information is in any case unlikely to be worth the time and effort involved in collecting it. If authorities do allow the CCRO access to computer systems held by other departments (which they are not obliged to do), then they must ensure that there are adequate security arrangements to prevent him/her from getting more from the system than names and addresses, and other information essential for compiling the register. It is vital that additional information is not removed from these systems and subsequently used for purposes relating to collection rather than registration.

On all these matters, local councils need to publish clear information on their policies and procedures. The relationship of trust between councils and the public will be placed under severe pressure; information is a vital tool in efforts to sustain such a relationship.

Responding to social security changes: protecting the poor

In devising a response to social security changes, local authorities are hampered by the fact that they have little control over the outcome. For example, the majority of housing benefit payments are made under statutory regulations laid down by the government. In this sense, the local authority merely acts as an agent for central government policies. However, two principles can usefully guide local authority actions in this area.

Administration

Firstly, they need to adopt best practice in relation to the administration of cash payments. This is becoming even more important as the role of local authorities shifts in emphasis away from the direct provision of housing and onto the administration of housing benefit. Best practice means providing widely available, clear information about eligibility, and processing claims quickly and correctly. Staff should have guidelines on the use of discretionary powers, with the emphasis on assisting the claimant where possible. Where rights of appeal or review are not obligatory, then ways of introducing them should be considered; where there are such rights — as with housing benefit review boards — they need to be advertised. Councils need to exploit the great advantage of local authority administration — the opportunity for genuine local accountability. Opportunities should be opened up for community groups and claimants to participate in decision-making over benefit matters. Where it has been tried, consultation of this sort over policies in discretionary areas, the design of publicity and the quality of administration has had an important effect on the standard of service provided.

Putting the claimant first

A second principle is that local authorities need to respond to government policy initiatives with the claimants' interests at the centre of their concerns. There are some unfortunate examples in recent years of local authorities failing to do this. The government proposals to introduce housing benefit were greeted with insufficient scepticism, because ironically many housing officials believed that the new scheme would reduce rent arrears. Moreover, local authority representatives actually opposed a right of appeal to an independent tribunal for housing benefit claimants. These are reminders that it is only too easy for large organisations to put their institutional interests before those of the people they serve: continuous vigilance is necessary to make sure this does not happen.

The division of responsibilities

The appropriate division of responsibility for social security between central and local government is a difficult issue. The Griffiths report on community care is an illustration of the issues at stake.

The Griffiths Report — and benefits

The Griffiths report, commissioned by the government, was published in March 1988.[4] The recommendations acknowledged the overwhelming case for local authorities taking a leading role in the organisation of community care. But Griffiths also recommended transferring the community care element of the social fund to local authorities; and replacing claimants' entitlement to income support for residential and nursing care with a basic level of housing benefit, topped up by discretionary payments made by local authorities. Moreover, these payments, along with all community care expenditure, would be at least 50 per cent funded from poll tax revenue. Thus claimants would move from having an entitlement, to reliance on discretionary payments — funded in large part from local revenue which will be severely restricted and insecure.

More than a year after receiving the report, the government had still not made a response. It was reported that the Prime Minister was opposed to giving local authorities additional responsibilities. Other ministers were in favour, because they were said to be satisfied that the poll tax would guarantee that expenditure on community care would remain severely limited.[5] The latest indications are that the latter view has prevailed.

On the local government side, there was a firm welcome for the proposal to give local authorities a leading role. But insufficient weight was given to other aspects of the proposals: in particular the proposals that entitlement to payments for residential care under income support should be removed, and that both community and residential care should be funded to a considerable extent out of the poll tax, have been firmly opposed by local authorities.

With the poll tax in place, there is a significant risk of local authorities being asked to shoulder responsibilities in the welfare field without adequate resources. As we have seen, the poll tax does not provide a stable and flexible source of revenue, and this is particularly so where needs may grow rapidly — as is the case, for example, with provision for the elderly. In our view, there is a clear case for some areas of social security provision which overlap with other local authority responsibilities — such as housing and community care — to be controlled locally. But, desirable though this may be, local authorities must be prepared to oppose proposals to devolve responsibilities where they cannot perform those responsibilities adequately — because of either the financial or the legal framework proposed. They should strongly resist proposals to substitute local discretion for statutory entitlement, and they should be clear that the poll tax can only provide at best a very small proportion of funding for new welfare responsibilities.

Claimants paying their way?

One specific policy question which is central to the issues we have dealt with in this book is that of minimum payments of local taxation. Should all claimants have to pay at least 20 per cent (or some other proportion) of local taxation?

It is worth noting at the outset that the principle that individuals must pay for what they vote for is not applied to national taxation. People on income support are unlikely to pay either income tax or national insurance. Even in the case of indirect taxes such as VAT, essentials such as food, children's clothing and fuel are exempt — a principle which the government has strongly defended in the light of moves by the European Economic Community to impose a uniform rate of tax on such items. It is true that the large increases in VAT since 1979 have substantially increased the national tax burden on claimants. But the concern with the payment of local taxation by all voters does not form part of a consistent approach to taxation policy by the government.

Nevertheless: inconsistent it may be, but is it right? There is an argument that the payment of some local taxation by all voters not only increases financial accountability but also enhances the status of claimants themselves. The crucial issue here is deciding the conditions which would make such a principle practicable. We find nothing objectionable in the principle that unemployed or elderly people should pay local taxation; what is deeply objectionable is that taxes should be levied from people too poor to pay them, resulting in the hardship we described in Chapter 4.

In our view, it is impractical for a tax which varies locally to be levied from those who rely on a subsistence benefit. There is no way (short of capping by central government, which removes local control) of guaranteeing that the level of the tax will not be set so high in a particular area as to reduce the incomes of claimants in that area below the subsistence level. Thus, if the idea of everyone 'paying their way' is an important objective, then the way of achieving it must be to increase the rates of insurance and universal benefits (as well as access to them) so that individuals have the money to be able to afford their local tax payments, without having their incomes reduced below the subsistence level. Of course, a subsistence level benefit would still be required, if only as a 'safety net', and anyone forced to rely on such a benefit should receive a 100 per cent rebate.

The case for universal benefits
Above all else, the distinctive feature of the April 1988 social security reforms was the attempt to demonstrate that means-tested benefits can successfully play a central role in social security provision. In this respect, the reforms must be judged a failure: they have not shown means-tested benefits to be capable of operating fairly or efficiently. There is no reason to expect that the changes will displace the deep-seated hostility of claimants themselves to this form of provision.

Attention, instead, should turn to methods of improving and extending universal benefits, which are popular, efficient and fair. Concerns about how state expenditure is 'targeted' in the end boil down to the question: who benefits? If this question is approached in the context of taxation as well as social security, then it is clear that universal state benefits can and do operate in such a way as to target spending on those in need. But they do so in a way which preserves the dignity and independence of recipients, and which is effective in terms of take-up.

Improving the poll tax

It is possible that the unfair nature of the poll tax will compel the government to take preventive action before it is introduced in England and Wales. The severity of the social security cuts when implemented caused such a political uproar that the government rushed to introduce some minor concessions. Ministers may well fear a repetition of this. If so, there are three obvious options they could pursue. Firstly, the government could increase the amount of grant paid either to all local authorities or specifically to those which face the highest poll tax levels. Secondly, the government could again improve the rebates scheme, perhaps by a further reduction in the taper. Finally, it could use capping powers to force lower poll tax levels in particular areas.

However, to sound a pessimistic warning, ministers have repeatedly stated that they are satisfied with the proposed new financial arrangements and rebates scheme. So — as with the bulk of the social security concessions made in April 1988 — any ameliorative action involving extra public spending may prove to be only temporary.

More importantly, each of these emergency measures would create problems of its own. Increasing the proportion of local authority spending covered by central government grant would make the 'gearing' effect even worse. An area which received more grant would, as a consequence, control a lower proportion of its own revenue. So the disproportionate effect of local spending decisions on the poll tax would be exaggerated still further by this measure. An improvement to the rebates scheme would increase the number of those eligible, with all the problems we have described in detail in Chapters 5 and 6. Capping individual authorities can hardly be presented as a measure to protect the poor: they would pay lower poll taxes, but at the cost of cuts in services. Moreover, direct central government control of poll tax levels jars with the government's main justification for the poll tax — that it will strengthen local democracy and accountability. It is symptomatic of the fundamental faults in the structure of the new system that action to ameliorate one aspect of the poll tax seems inevitably to make other defects even worse.

Alternatives to the poll tax

We do not intend here to enter into a technical evauation of the various options for local taxation. But it is worth considering whether there are alternatives which meet certain basic requirements.

The government has argued that there is no such alternative, and that everyone agrees that the rates should be abolished. Yet, while it is correct to criticise the rates for being regressive and falling harshly on single-person households, one of the conclusions of this book is that the rates are in fact preferable to the poll tax as a system of local taxation. There are few criticisms of the rates as a tax on business property; and indeed the government itself is retaining the business rate while centralising control over it.

The domestic rates are better related to ability to pay than the poll tax (although insufficiently so). They also have the great merit of taxing domestic property: the removal of such a tax creates the absurd situation in which owner-occupiers get tax relief in respect of their properties (mortgage interest tax relief) while not paying tax on them in any way; it is also likely to inflate property prices. However, the arguments for a tax on privately-owned domestic property do not entail that such a tax should be payable by tenants, nor that such a tax should be the main source of local revenue (it could equally be a central government tax).

We suggest some principles which could underlie an acceptable form of local taxation. The principles for fairness in local taxation which have been adopted by many national voluntary organisations, charities and church groups who formed the 'Poll Tax Forum' early in 1989 are in the box below.

Either a local income tax or rates, or a combination of the two, could be designed as domestic taxes to meet the requirements set out in the Charter (see box). The rates are less well related to ability to pay, and arguably go beyond a tax on wealth when they fall on tenants. On the other hand, they score highly on an important

---

CHARTER FOR A FAIR LOCAL TAX

'A fair system of local taxation should be based on the following principles:

- **Ability to pay**

A fair tax should be based on the taxpayer's income and/or wealth. In addition, there should be an adequate, simple rebate scheme to ensure that local taxation does not cause hardship to people on low incomes.

- **Confidentiality**

Local tax should be collected without abusing principles of confidentiality. Personal information required for administering tax should not be disclosed to third parties. Information supplied to statutory authorities for purposes mainly unrelated to taxation should not be used in the collection of tax.

- **Local democracy**

The level of local tax should be determined by locally elected representatives in relation to local needs and without central government control. Local services are of benefit to both local residents and businesses: both sections of the community should contribute directly to locally determined taxation.

- **The right to vote**

The operation of local tax should not be such as to discourage people from voting.

- **Additional funding for local needs**

Central government should use the national system to provide grants to local authorities, to supplement revenues from local tax. Central government grants should aim to equalise the position of local authorities, taking account of the variations of needs and resources between areas.'

criterion not directly relevant to the issue of fairness addressed by these principles — the ease of collection and the security of revenue for service provision. Income tax is harder to collect, and easier to evade — but is better related to ability to pay. In either case, each would need to be supplemented by a locally controlled business tax — probably the rates — and an adequate national grant system based on resources and needs. We have seen the crippling effect, especially on deprived areas, of a failure to meet these requirements.

Conclusion

Going back over the principles relating to fairness listed in the box, the poll tax fails on every count, wholly or in part. We have argued that action to improve the poll tax, for example by increasing the level of central government grant, cannot deal with its fundamental faults as a local tax. The only appropriate response to these faults is to look for an alternative form of local taxation based on ability to pay, which is capable of providing a secure base for spending on local welfare.

As far as benefits are concerned, the government should abandon its attempt to expand the role of discretionary means-tested benefits. Instead it should seek to strengthen the universal benefits, based on entitlement. These benefits can operate fairly and efficiently in conjunction with a more redistributive system of national taxation. Local authorities need to emphasise these principles in response to government proposals to further reforms of social security — especially when such proposals involve a role for local authorities in the administration of benefits.

Local authorities are, however, faced with the necessity of implementing government legislation. In practice, they *must* collect the poll tax, albeit under protest. So they must also take what steps are possible to protect local services and the poor. This means reviewing collection procedures and administrative arrangements; and basing budgetary decisions on far more detailed knowledge of how services are distributed within the community than has been necessary in the past.

Notes

1 Glen Bramley, Julian Le Grand and William Low,'How far is the poll tax a "community charge"? The implications of service usage', Discussion Paper WSP/42, April 1989 (The Welfare State Programme, ST/ICERD, London School of Economics). The authors include two estimates of poll tax payments net of rebates.
2 *Paying for Local Government*, Green Paper, Cmnd 9714, HMSO, January 1986.
3 Although in the English and Welsh shire counties the poll tax is to be collected at the district level, while social services is a county function.
4 Sir Roy Griffiths, *Community Care — agenda for action*, HMSO, London, 1988.
5 *Sunday Telegraph*, 26 March 1989.

12 Conclusion

We have examined the effects of the poll tax and recent changes to social security alongside each other. We have found that the recent social security changes tend to act in concert with the poll tax. Both redistribute income from the poor to the better-off; both promise the protection of means-tested benefits to the poor, but fail to deliver the goods; both hold out hopes for greater individual freedom and independence, for a shift in power from the state to the individual, yet both subject individuals who rely on state provision to greater bureaucracy and to a diminution of rights.

We have argued that help from the state, whether in the form of cash benefits or local authority services, is very often the prerequisite of independence. All of us are dependent on help from the state, whether it is in the form of benefits, tax relief or services. It is not the fact that these are provided by the state which infringes personal freedom and choice, but the form, nature and manner in which they are provided.

One objective of the social security reforms has been to free individuals from the 'culture of dependency' by targeting help on the poorest through means-tested benefits. People would be encouraged to become self-reliant through making private provision for themselves. The primary aim of the poll tax is to increase the accountability of local authorities to their voters. The government has argued that the individual flat-rate tax is fairer than rates and efficient to administer. It will require each voter to make a financial contribution to their local authority. The relationship between local spending and the level of the poll tax is supposed to be comprehensible and visible. Moreover, the poll tax is an individual 'charge' for the use of services — hence the name 'community charge'.

Both changes aim at a shrinking of government activity. In social security state support has been identified as encouraging 'dependency', whereas private provision is seen as the means to 'independence'. Thus the aim is to restrict state help to the neediest only. The government expects the poll tax and the changes to local authority finance to exert a downward pressure on service spending — thus freeing individuals from the 'shackles of local government'.

But, as this book has demonstrated, these ideals could hardly be further from the reality.

The 1988 social security reforms (in conjunction with tax changes) have not targeted resources on the poorest; instead they have transferred them to the affluent. Many aspects of the changes — the increase in discretion, the spread of complex means-tested benefits and the cash losses — have served to increase rather than decrease dependency.

As part of the social security changes, everyone, no matter how poor, has had to pay 20 per cent of their rates. This measure was a forerunner of the poll tax, embodying the government's principle of 'accountability' — that everyone should make a financial contribution to local authorities. But, rather than enhancing accountability, the extra costs for claimants have caused hardship, insecurity and anxiety.

The poll tax is intrinsically unfair — as a flat-rate tax, it falls equally on the shoulders of the rich and the poor. Even with the help of rebates it is poorly related to the ability to pay. Whichever way the impact of the poll tax is measured (with and without the changes to the rebate scheme), it is more regressive than the rating system. It brings cuts in living standards for nearly all but the well-off.

The number of people on poll tax rebates soars because so many cannot afford the burdensome tax. But rebates are saddled with the same problems that beset other means-tested benefits — they are complex, intrusive and very often not claimed by those entitled to them. They are incapable of the task assigned to them — to protect the poor from the operation of the market principle in local authority finance through the introduction of a flat-rate 'charge'. The 'near-poor' fall outside the scope of rebates and many of the very poorest will simply slip through the net of protection. And how long will it be before poll tax rebates face the same fate as housing benefit, which has been cut so savagely in recent years?

The reform of local government finance sharply penalises spending on services. These services are crucial to the living standards of low-income groups. The reforms involve a substantial shift in resources from deprived to non-deprived regions, leaving the poorest regions to bear the highest poll taxes. This pattern is repeated among individual authorities. Moreover, the problem of 'gearing' (where increases in local authority spending fall disproportionately on residents) afflicts the deprived authorities most severely. There, where services are most needed, it will be more costly to sustain services at their current level, let alone improve them.

Local authorities have a major and continuing role in providing services and benefits. There is as yet no indication that these responsibilities are diminishing. However, the government is making it increasingly difficult for authorities to carry out these responsibilities adequately. The poll tax and social security changes have reinforced that pattern: local authorities are given new responsibilities, but the powers and resources to carry them out are restricted.

The implementation of the poll tax comes with a vast increase in bureaucracy and new powers of enforcement. Local authorities have been landed with the nightmarish responsibility of administering a complex rebate scheme which aims to protect the poor from a highly regressive tax. Far from increasing individual power, the poll tax brings with it an army of powers: direct deductions from benefit and earnings, enforcement of joint and several liability and the cohabitation rule, the use of information from personal records, to name just some of them. The poll tax systematically infringes the principles of confidentiality, independence and democracy.

The analogy between the 'community charge' and the market place is largely spurious. The poll tax is not related to the use of services. It is a compulsory tax, set by local authorities, which are elected periodically. It bears little relation to paying for goods in the market place. Instead of taking refuge in false analogies, and terms such as 'community charge', the government should address the serious and important issue of how to make local authority services more accountable to the public.

We hope that the search for alternatives—both short and long term — to these measures soon gathers strength. Approaches to welfare in the 1980s have been conditioned by the priorities of restricting the role of the state and curbing state expenditure. Alternative approaches are likely to rest on notions of citizenship and participation — a form of welfare which places a premium on fairness and minimum standards. In relation to local taxation, that means placing ability to pay at the heart of the objectives pursued in the next round of reforms. For social security it means an emphasis on the rights of the individual — an assertion of the benefits of entitlement rather than discretion; and it means an extension of the scope of universal benefits to bring about a less divided society.

Certainly local authorities have a vital role to play in the provision of local welfare in the 1990s. In order to play that role, they must themselves demonstrate a determination to do what is possible to protect their communities from the divisive impact of recent central government policies. Harder still, they must seek to preserve services of quality in the face of the considerable destructive pressures which are bearing down upon them.

Appendices

APPENDIX 1
Scottish local authorities – deprivation ratios and poll tax levels

Authority	Deprivation ratio[1]	Poll tax[2]	Implied poll tax (without safety nets)[3]
Glasgow	3.16	306	361
Monklands	2.89	293	300
Inverclyde	2.28	291	291
Clydebank	2.11	297	315
Motherwell	1.72	305	305
Hamilton	1.61	291	296
Dundee	1.38	324	321
Renfrew	1.30	295	308
Dumbarton	1.27	298	321
Cunninghame	0.96	278	308
Cumnock & Doon Valley	0.89	276	296
Edinburgh	0.82	392	384
West Lothian	0.76	359	353
Kilmarnock & Loudoun	0.75	269	289
Western Isles	0.63	171	171
Stirling	0.56	310	275
Clackmannan	0.44	300	266
Kirkcaldy	0.44	298	293
Strathkelvin	0.43	299	301
Nithsdale	0.42	245.5	215
Inverness	0.36	226	200
Dunfermline	0.36	293	293
Kyle & Carrick	0.35	308	308
Cumbernauld & Kilsyth	0.30	275	292
Aberdeen	0.28	304	272
Lochaber	0.25	237	216
Roxburgh	0.25	247	211
Skye & Lochalsh	0.25	225	204
Wigtown	0.25	246.5	205
Banff & Buchan	0.24	275.7	238
Perth & Kinross	0.22	299	277
Sutherland	0.20	206	161
Clydesdale	0.18	301	311
Caithness	0.17	225	213
Argyll & Bute	0.17	277	301
Angus	0.15	293	280
Annandale & Eskdale	0.13	253.5	229
East Lothian	0.12	374	360
Ross & Cromarty	0.09	239	207
North-East Fife	0.07	320	303
Midlothian	0.06	364	367
Moray	0.06	261	219
Falkirk	0.04	259	221

Authority	Deprivation ratio[1]	Poll tax[2]	Implied poll tax (without safety nets)[3]
Nairn	0	228	196
Stewarty	0	243.5	218
Bearsden & Milngavie	0	298	291
Ettrick & Lauderdale	0	247	202
Badenoch & Strathspey	0	235	209
Gordon	0	263	224
East Kilbride	0	318	324
Orkney	0	248	209
Eastwood	0	282	280
Kincardine & Deeside	0	251	196
Tweeddale	0	248	197
Shetland	0	114.16	114
Berwickshire	0	236	190

Notes
1 For calculation of the 'deprivation ratio', see note 2 to Chapter 9.
2 The poll tax levels charged from April 1989, including water charges.
3 The poll tax levels charged from April 1989, with an adjustment to exclude the effects of safety nets.

APPENDIX 2
Fifty deprived English authorities and poll tax levels

Authority	Z-score[1]	Poll tax[2]
Hackney	6.69	578
Newham	5.84	284
Tower Hamlets	5.53	616
Lambeth	5.52	490
Hammersmith	4.98	473
Haringey	4.86	291
Islington	4.80	480
Brent	4.62	307
Wandsworth	4.50	397
Southwark	4.40	515
Manchester	4.19	285
Camden	4.05	639
Leicester	4.02	232
Wolverhampton	3.77	240
Liverpool	3.51	284
Birmingham	3.51	218
Lewisham	3.46	577
Kensington	3.34	340
Coventry	3.17	248
Sandwell	3.15	258
Nottingham	3.14	251

Authority	Z-score[1]	Poll tax[2]
Waltham Forest	3.09	269
Blackburn	3.08	251
Westminster	2.97	373
Ealing	2.94	234
Knowsley	2.67	282
Middlesbrough	2.62	282
Slough	2.44	178
Preston	2.41	243
Scunthorpe	2.34	306
Kingston-upon-Hull	2.30	268
Bradford	2.22	277
Corby	2.14	217
Burnley	2.10	279
Greenwich	2.08	589
Rochdale	2.05	278
Brighton	1.99	202
Salford	1.96	273
Hove	1.93	198
Luton	1.87	249
Oxford	1.82	283
Hastings	1.81	196
Derwentside	1.79	279
Stoke-on-Trent	1.75	214
Kirklees	1.69	289
Oldham	1.69	225
Hounslow	1.68	243
Tameside	1.63	276
South Tyneside	1.63	267
Walsall	1.60	268

Notes
1   See note 6 to Chapter 9.
2   Department of the Environment projected poll tax levels for 1988/89
    (without safety nets).

APPENDIX 3
Fifty non-deprived English authorities and poll tax levels

Authority	Z-score (negative)[1]	Poll tax[2]
Ryedale	4.39	205
Wokingham	4.14	208
Craven	4.10	213
Richmondshire	4.08	211
Hambleton	4.08	208
Hart	3.88	216
Harborough	3.84	216
Daventry	3.75	240

Authority	Z-score (negative)[1]	Poll tax[2]
Castle Morpeth	3.72	254
South Northants	3.71	207
Rutland	3.68	199
Derby Dales	3.61	267
South Derbyshire	3.56	261
Epsom & Ewell	3.52	220
Harrogate	3.47	235
Selby	3.45	227
Mid Beds	3.42	252
East Herts	3.42	246
Surrey Heath	3.42	189
South Cambs	3.42	186
Eden	3.41	256
Ribble Valley	3.41	236
Chiltern	3.38	234
Mole Valley	3.38	173
Northavon	3.37	254
Kingswood	3.37	240
Uttlesford	3.36	225
Basingstoke	3.33	178
Broadland	3.32	179
Mid Sussex	3.31	180
Brentwood	3.30	384
Eastleigh	3.30	188
Rushcliffe	3.23	244
Stratford	3.12	229
Tewkesbury	3.12	198
Rochford	3.11	224
East Dorset	3.11	180
South Lakeland	3.10	263
South Bucks	3.04	235
Mid Suffolk	3.03	199
Test Valley	3.03	186
Kennet	3.01	220
Wansdyke	2.98	234
South Norfolk	2.97	178
Horsham	2.96	180
Vale of White Horse	2.92	231
Newbury	2.91	176
Beverley	2.88	263
Elmbridge	2.86	189
Bracknell	2.84	172

Notes
1 See note 6 to Chapter 9.
2 Department of the Environment projected poll tax levels for 1988/89
   (without safety nets).

Index